FAMILY GROWTH

ELECTIVES

Growing Together
with
Your Teens

Studies for Parents of Teens

Dave and Neta Jackson

David C. Cook Publishing Co., Elgin, Illinois—Weston, Ontario

850 N. Grove Ave., Elgin, IL 60120-2892
Cable address: DCCOOK
Cover designer: Tom Schild
Cover illustrator: Pete Whyte
Illustrator: Julian Jackson
Desktop published by Dave and Neta Jackson
Printed in U.S.A.

ISBN: 0-7814-5023-3

Contents

Welcome to Family Growth Electives

Congratulations! The fact that you are using a study in the Family Growth Electives series says that you are concerned about today's families. You and your group of adults are about to begin an exciting adventure.

Each course in this series has been created with today's families in mind. Rather than taking a single topic and applying it to all adults, these Family Growth Electives treat each adult life stage separately. This means that people who are approaching or going through similar stages in life can get together to share and study their common needs from a biblical perspective.

The concept of family life stages comes from the work of Dr. Dennis B. Guernsey, associate professor of Marital and Family Therapy, Fuller Theological Seminary. Guernsey says that the family has critical tasks to accomplish at each stage in order to nurture healthy Christians.

Many adults in churches today have not come from strong Christian roots. Others may have attended church as children, drifted away during their adolescent or young adult years, and are now back in church in an effort to get help with the everyday problems of family life.

Some adults do not have the benefits of living near their extended family. The church can meet the needs of such people by becoming their "family." It can also help strengthen families by teaching them biblical principles and giving opportunities for applying those principles. That's exactly what you'll be doing as you lead your group in this Family Growth Electives study.

Terri Hibbard, Editor

Reconvene the whole group and ask: **What is the Bible trying to say to us through David's struggles in these areas?** (Responses might include: God involves Himself in the life choices and transitions we make. If we make wise choices, His blessing is with us. There are consequences for poor or sinful choices. It is important to seek God whenever we face major decisions. It is possible to get off track later in life.)

Mention that there are many other passages in the Bible that speak to the major challenges of mid-life: problems of good and bad marriages, self-esteem, life purpose, work, grief, interactions with children and older parents, spiritual maturity, impatience, physical illness, disappointment, and so on. The Book of Proverbs, especially, has some frank advice for selecting friends, making wise choices, practicing responsible sexuality, developing good character, and charting a positive life direction. While these and similar issues are rarely referenced to age, biblical teachings apply universally; we must discover how they meet our unique needs at each stage of life.

❸ Issues Common to Parents and Teens

Objective:
To identify both mid-life and adolescent issues
(10 minutes).

Distribute copies of "The Middlescence/Adolescence Stress Scales" (RS-1B). Invite the parents to fill out both halves, for themselves and for their teens. If some have more than one adolescent, provide extra copies to fill out later.

Allow about seven minutes for the group members to fill out the sheet, and then discuss the following questions.
- **What impressed you most about the amount of stress or lack of it in your life?**
- **In the life of your teenager?**
- **Compare the life events in the adult and the teen columns. What are the most notable similarities between what adults and adolescents might face?**

❹ Back to Basics

Objective:
To encourage parents to write a prayer that helps them identify their greatest needs, fears, and hopes
(10-25 minutes).

Explain that the University of Minnesota Center for Youth Development and Research has examined the collision between adolescence and middlescence and has concluded that both groups are having some of the same problems at the same time.

Erase the board and draw a line down the middle. At the top of the left column write, "Mid-Life," and on the right,

"Adolescence." Then record on the left the group's responses to the question: **We have looked at a list of possible specific stresses, but what are the major categories faced by mid-life adults?** Try to list at least five issues. **What are the major developmental issues faced by adolescents?** Record the answers in the right column.

Draw lines between complementary issues faced by both teens and mid-life adults. Explore with the group the similarities and differences between the ways parents and teens wrestle with similar issues. Guide the group only enough to be sure the following categories[2] are mentioned in some way during the discussion:

- **Body changes.** Adolescents' bodies are changing via rapid development, while the energy available in middle-aged bodies becomes definitely limited. Death, for mid-life adults, is no longer a "ridiculous abstraction."
- **Sexuality.** Parents who may be fearing menopause or experiencing periods of psychological impotence, may envy their adolescents who are struggling to adjust to their maturing sexuality.
- **Vocation.** Teenagers face difficult choices for the future, while their mid-life parents may be haunted by unachieved career goals, unfulfilled dreams, and bad choices. Each group may feel a threat from the other in the job market.
- **Family roles.** On the surface, adolescents are eager for complete freedom, and their parents may long for peace and quiet. But underneath there can be dread of the "empty nest" and facing the cold, cruel world on one's own. Some homemakers may sense a not-so-subtle cultural message that they may have wasted their lives and missed out on a career. Fathers often want to turn back to the family just at the time their children are demanding more distance.

Circle these four issues on the board (or the group's equivalent wording for the same categories), and explain that these four issues will be among the things addressed in future sessions.

Distribute copies of "A Prayer of Hope" (RS-1C) and blank sheets of paper to any who need them.

We have seen how King David encountered several life stages—some triumphantly and some tragically—and yet, with all of David's problems, God could still say

With all of David's problems, God could still say he was "a man after my own heart."

he was "a man after my own heart" (Acts 13:22). One reason was David's honesty in taking his problems and feelings to the Lord, as recorded for us in many of the psalms.

The psalms often follow a poetic style in which David states the problem, verbalizes his feelings, describes how he wants the Lord to help him, expresses his doubts and fears, and then places his trust in the Lord again.

In this course, we want to anticipate both the positive and negative aspects of this middle period of life. As we explore the potential problems, we will grow stronger by bringing them to the Lord.

Encourage the group members to complete the five exercises at the top of the page before they turn the page upside down to read the application instructions. If you are short on time, have the parents do this activity at home.

After the group members finish writing, ask the group members to divide into teams of three in which they can share their Prayers of Hope and pray for one another. Encourage those in the small groups to exchange names and phone numbers and to phone each other in the weeks ahead to ask for or offer additional prayer.

Close the session with a prayer of blessing on the group as you explore these important issues in the weeks ahead.

Notes:

1. "The New Middle Age," *Newsweek*, Dec. 7, 1992, 52.
2. Charles Bradshaw, *You and Your Teen* (Elgin, Ill.: David C. Cook Publishing Co., 1985), 12.

Living with Purpose

2

Session Aim:
To show the need for reassessing one's purpose and goals at mid-life and to give opportunity to do that.

Responsibilities for most men and women in their middle years are staggering. The last session focused on the growing tensions with the younger generation, but there is another generation that puts the squeeze on mid-life plans: grandparents. Children may be venturing into independence, but grandparents are approaching a time when they may need more attention.

Mid-life is a "sandwich population," said Dr. Virginia Boyack, a gerontologist and vice president of California Federal Savings and Loan. "You're being pulled by generations on both sides."

It is also a time of accountability to one's self. We come to realize whether or not our life values have been valid. By this time, most of us have achieved many material and vocational goals or have accepted the fact that we're not going to reach them. Jobs become more secure because of experience . . . or more insecure because old skills become obsolete and younger, lower paid workers are available.

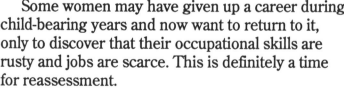

Some women may have given up a career during child-bearing years and now want to return to it, only to discover that their occupational skills are rusty and jobs are scarce. This is definitely a time for reassessment.

—Charles Bradshaw

Mid-life is a sandwich population; you're pulled by generations on both sides."

Getting Ready

Scriptures:
Psalm 90:12; Matthew 25:14-30; I Corinthians 9:24, 26; Proverbs 13:19; Ephesians 5:15-17.

1. Reproduce copies of "Where I Thought I Was Going" (RS-2A), "Living with Purpose" (RS-2B), "My Mission Statement" (RS-2C), and "Stepping-Stones" (RS-2D).
2. On your chalkboard or a sheet of newsprint write the following statement. Then cover it or turn it so the group will not see it until you wrap up the session.

> **Some people are afraid to set goals for fear that they may fail. Others are afraid to set goals because they feel that to do so would hinder the work of the Holy Spirit. The first is a failure to trust God to work. The second is a failure to realize that God expects us to be about His business.**

❶ Once Upon a Time

Objective:
To help the group members recall the goals they had in younger years as a basis for reevaluating their present life directions (10 minutes).

Begin the session by asking how many of the group members have seriously reevaluated their life achievements and direction in recent years. Ask for volunteers to describe what areas of life they have reevaluated and whether it led them to make any course changes. After each person shares, ask for a show of hands from others who have reevaluated that same area.

Distribute copies of RS-2A, "Where I Thought I Was Going." Talk the group through questions one and two, inviting as many people as possible to set the stage to times past. The members will undoubtedly enjoy laughing at some fads and concerns of earlier years. After a few minutes, have them privately answer the other questions on the resource sheet.

❷ Living with Purpose

Objective:
To establish the need for reevaluating and refocusing one's purpose in life (10 minutes).

See if the group members can identify the source of the following quote:

> **"Would you tell me please, which way I ought to go from here?"**
> **"That depends a good deal on where you want to get to."**
> **"I don't much care where."**
> **"Then it doesn't matter which way you go."**

(The quote is an exchange between Alice and the Cheshire Cat from Lewis Carroll's *Alice in Wonderland*.)

T *ell me please, which way I ought to go from here?"*

Ask someone to look up and read Psalm 90:12 ("Teach us to number our days aright, that we may gain a heart of wisdom"), and ask the parents what they think this means in light of the quote from *Alice in Wonderland*.

Alice lacked purpose, so she lacked the ability to ask for directions. The Psalmist encourages us to think about our purpose in life by numbering our days, so we can wisely determine direction or adjust for the time we have left. This is one of the things people in mid-life do naturally. We start counting the years we have left, instead of the number of years lived. While doing this, it is important to take an inventory of our life purpose.

Divide the group into teams of three to do a brief Bible study on Jesus' parable of the talents in Matthew 25:14-30. Distribute copies of "Living with Purpose" (RS-2B), and encourage the triads to work through the questions.

When the group comes back together, emphasize: **Sometimes we think industrious people must be selfish—out to get it all, but it really depends upon motives. In this parable, the third servant, the who buried his one talent, was actually the selfish one. He was merely looking out for number one, unwilling to risk his well-being for the benefit of the master.**

❸ *Purpose* or *Goals*?

Objective:
To help the group note the differences between a life purpose and intermediate goals (5 minutes).

Based on the Bible study they have just done and upon their own perspective, invite the group to try and define purpose and distinguish it from goals. Write responses on the chalk or marker board.

The distinctions should include the following:

Purposes
- Like a company's mission statement.
- The overall direction.
- Includes vision, dreams.
- How I want to be remembered.
- What I want to have contributed when my life is over.
- Purpose should be an enduring objective.
- Living out God's will for me.

Goals
- Steps by which I achieve my purpose.
- They should be specific and measurable.
- Good goals must be realistic.
- Goals may get refined frequently.

When the group has reached a satisfactory distinction between purpose and goals, test their agreement by asking which of the following they would be define as a purpose and which would be a goal.
- **I want to get a base hit this inning.** *(Goal.)*
- **I want to raise my batting average to 325 this year.** *(Goal.)*
- **I want to become a good ball player.** *(Purpose.)*

Offer other examples as appropriate, while noting that both short- and long-term goals are necessary in achieving our life purpose. Emphasize that whether short- or long-term, good goals need to be specific and measurable.

❹ Identifying My Purposes and Goals

Objective:
To assist group members in reviewing and defining their purposes for life and the goals by which they hope to achieve them (15-30 minutes).

Hand out copies of "My Mission Statement" (RS-2C), and instruct the group members to work individually, writing a purpose for each area indicated. Once the parents have written a prospective purpose for each area, they should test it with a partner (other than their spouse), not for merit but to determine whether what they have written is a purpose and not a goal.

Refining purposes into a mission statement is more challenging. Instruct the group members that they should think about the concept in the week to come, taking at least a full hour to continue reassessing their purposes and developing a mission statement. The objective in this session is to stimulate serious consideration more than to conclude a statement.

As time allows, have the group members continue working on their mission statements. Reconvene the group and ask volunteers to read what they have come up with to encourage others.

Then share the following perspective:

For the Christian, the secret of managing life is to define prayerfully what kind of a life you believe God wants you to lead and where you fit in His strategy. This is your mission statement with its component purposes.

When we divide life's journey into segments, we can tell where we've been, how far we've come, and where we're going.

But then you should set specific goals for things that will help you fulfill those purposes. It has been shown repeatedly that the person who has clear, strong goals is the person who lives the most effective life.

If we haven't set any goals, if we haven't established some milestones along the path, then we won't know where we are. But when we divide the journey into specific segments, we can tell where we've been, how far we've come, and where we're going.

As you distribute copies of "Stepping-Stones" (RS-2D), continue to explain: **There are two kinds of goals in life—long-range and short-range. Long-range goals refer to things we want to accomplish in our lives eventually. Such goals can be general but should be as realistic as possible (e.g., "I want to be a good teacher" is better than "I want to be awarded the 'Best Teacher in the U.S.' award"). Keep your long-range goals flexible so you won't feel a sense of frustration and failure if you don't achieve them.**

Then set short-range goals that are realistic, specific, and designed to help you reach your long-range goals. Remember that you will fail at these goals sometimes. When this happens, evaluate what went wrong, reset your goal, and try again. When you achieve a goal, have a celebration. Reward yourself in some way and then push on to accomplish the next short-range goal.

Based on their purposes in six areas of life, instruct group members to select one long-term and one short-term goal for each purpose and write it out on the resource sheet. The short-term goal should be a direct stepping-stone for achieving the long-term goal.

Tell the group members to bring this resource sheet to the next session for one of the activities.

❺ Wrap Up

Objective:
To review the importance of establishing purpose and goals in our own lives and in relation to our children (5 minutes).

Reveal the statement (given in the Getting Ready section) that you wrote on the chalkboard or sheet of newsprint, and invite the group to discuss whether or not it is true.

To conclude, ask the group members to discuss: **What impact do you think your personal purpose and goal setting has had on your adolescent?**

When you fail, evaluate what went wrong, reset your goal, and try again.

- In the area of stress management?
- Personal identity?
- Career development?
- Marriage stability?
- Spiritual maturity?

Close the session by praying that God will help each of the parents more clearly understand his or her purpose in life and find effective ways of moving toward that purpose.

Easing The Load of Mid-Life

3

Session Aim:
To encourage the group members to prioritize their goals so they can be role models to their teens and make their mid-life transition smoother.

In the first session the group saw that the mid-life transition represents a developmental link between early adulthood and middle adulthood and is part of both eras. It represents a beginning and an ending, a meeting of past and future. Threads of obligation often trap mid-life people—responsibility, hopes, dreams, and ambitions that make up a network of interdependence and expectations. They are at neither the beginning nor the end of life . . . of family, of marriage, or work, of all the major roles of adulthood.

Parents in mid-life are responsible for generations on both sides. Children not yet launched require a delicate balance of freedom and supervision. Grandparents may be needing increased assistance and companionship.

The transition through mid-life may be relatively smooth, but it commonly involves considerable turmoil. This is not dependent upon a person's previous success or failure in achieving goals, but upon the ability to re-evaluate and adjust goals during mid-life. At this time it becomes particularly important to ask: "What have I done with my life? What do I really get from and give to my wife, children, friends, work, church, and self? What is it I truly want for myself and others?" One task of mid-life is to work on and resolve the discrepancy between what is and what might be.

—Charles Bradshaw

One task of mid-life is to resolve the discrepancy between what is and what might be.

Getting Ready

Scriptures:
Matthew 11:28-30; 6:19-34;
Proverbs 15:22; 21:31

1. Prepare two copies of "Christmas Classics" (RS-3A) for the volunteers who will read the summaries to the group.
2. Photocopy "The Easy Yoke" (RS-3B) for each participant. But make three copies each of "A Sample Plan" (RS-3C) for each group member. Make a few extra copies of "Stepping-Stones" (RS-2D) from last session.
3. Write the following "Priority Test Questions" on a chalk or marker board. If possible, cover them or turn them so they will not distract the parents until you need them.

- How urgent is it?
- How important is it?
- How often must it be done?
- Can someone else do it?
- Is it part of a larger purpose to which I am committed?
- What will happen if it is not done at all?
- Is it realistic? Can it be done?

❶ Weighed in the Balance

Objective:
To help the group members realize the benefit of evaluating their priorities in order to help adjust to mid-life (15 minutes).

Most of the group will be able to recall two classic Christmas stories that are retold almost every year: *A Christmas Carol* by Charles Dickens and *It's a Wonderful Life*, the 1946 motion picture starring Jimmy Stewart.

Pass out one copy each of "Christmas Classics" (RS-3A) to two volunteers and have each read one of the summaries to the group. Don't let the group digress into discussing the theological accuracy of details in either story.

In both stories, the principal character reviews his life upon the occasion of facing death. What is the primary contrast between them? (The answers should highlight that Ebenezer Scrooge had lived a selfish life, and his review inspired him to repent and make major changes in his priorities. George Bailey, on the other hand, had served others his whole life long but felt discouraged because he saw no value in what he had done. His review changed his perspective, encouraged him to keep on living, and affirmed his previous priorities.)

What are the similarities between how these two men experienced their process of evaluation? (Neither enjoyed the process—the test—but both appreciated the results. Point out that often we fear evaluations, but whether we are called to change or reaffirm previous priorities, the results can be rewarding. Ebenezer Scrooge, who was weighed in the balance and found wanting, was nonetheless delighted with life once he made the required changes. George Bailey, who was called to recommitment, did so with tremendous joy instead of his earlier suicidal melancholy.)

Whether we need to make a course correction or recommit ourselves to our previous directions, getting our priorities straight can smooth our mid-life transitions and energize us for years to come.

❷ The Real Priorities

Objective:
To help the group members consider how important their goals would be to them if they only had six months to live (10 minutes).

Tell the group members to picture the following situation:

Imagine that you have only six months to live. You will not have any pain, but you know that you will die in six months. This means that you must squeeze whatever you consider important into six months. Before you start thinking about it, assume that you have attended to everything related to your death: completed your will, bought a cemetery plot, settled all your affairs. Now think about the long- and short-term goals you established last session. How would you prioritize them? What other priorities would you add to what you want to do during these last six months? Would your short-term goals be any different? Be honest.

Divide the group into several teams to discuss this question for five minutes. After five minutes, ask for general feedback from the discussion. Many will find their goals will change. Usually, their goals will become more relational. People will desire to spend more time with people. (Note that this does not mean that previous goals, set with the assumption of living several more years, are invalid—but rather it identifies some important goals that may be missing.)

❸ Eternity's Values

Objective:
To discover the biblical basis for adjusting our priorities to ease our burden (10 minutes).

Ask a volunteer to read Matthew 11:28-30 where Jesus promises that His yoke is easy and His burden is light. Then ask:

- **How many of you would like an easier yoke and a lighter burden at this time in your life?**
- **What constitutes an easy yoke and a light burden?**

(One that suits the gifts and strength God has given us.)

- **Was Jesus just speaking of relative "ease" to get us to appreciate that our lot in life is not as hard as those who are starving, in prison, or living in the midst of war? Or did He really mean "light" and "easy"?** (An "easy" time of it, actually or relatively, is not the point. The Bible says that we will face suffering and hardship in the Christian life, but it is not too heavy. See II Cor. 12:9.)
- **How can we exchange our heavy burdens for lighter ones?** (Make sure we are doing only what God wants us to do.)

The group will probably agree that the secret to a light and easy burden is selecting the right priorities in life by taking on Jesus' yoke—that is, doing God's will rather than pursuing our own agenda.

Answers to sheets

Distribute copies of "The Easy Yoke" (RS-3B) and divide the group into teams of about four people each to work through the Bible study questions. (If needed, the answers are: 1—accumulating earthly treasures, worrying about physical needs and the future; 2—treasures in heaven; 3—they are insecure and we cannot change some things; 4—they will consume our attention; 5—it is not possible; 6—God will provide all our needs.)

---

❹ Evaluating Priorities

Objective:
To help the group members evaluate goal priorities (5 minutes).

Scripture tells us to seek first the kingdom of God—a priority that will ease our mid-life transitions. But even when that is our heart's intention, how do we evaluate the specific demands for our daily attention?

Display the chalk or marker board on which you previously wrote the "Priority Test Questions" and talk the group through them. Encourage group members to share examples of when they have used any of these questions. Also have them take notes. To stimulate contributions, you might ask: **Why is this an important test?** The following are comments you might add if the discussion lags.

- **How urgent is it?** General Eisenhower once said, "The urgent is seldom important, and the important is seldom urgent." Too many of us enjoy putting out little fires. "Fire fighting" can become a major distraction from the more important issues we'd rather not face.

*T*he urgent is seldom important, and the important is seldom urgent."

- **How important is it?** Not everything is important. Great chunks of life are routine and monotonous. But some things should be important, and if we're doing nothing that is important to us, we may soon conclude that we are unimportant people. This often happens at mid-life.
- **How often must it be done?** There are some things that we need to do regularly. They are molehills that could become mountains if they are not tended to on a timely basis.
- **Can someone else do it more effectively than I?** Perhaps the answer is no or maybe, in which case the task may be your responsibility. However, if the answer is yes, then perhaps this shouldn't be one of your priorities at all.
- **Is it part of a larger purpose to which I am committed?** This question relates to our life purposes and goals.
- **What will happen if it is not done at all?** (Another way of asking this is, "How important will this be in twenty years?") Will there be a disaster? or nothing? If the answer is nothing, maybe that's a clue to give it a low priority. To "Never put off until tomorrow what you can do today" is great—unless what we're doing today distracts us from our long-term goal or larger purpose.
- **Is it realistic?** Much of human behavior is self-defeating. We want to succeed, but we set goals so high that we are sure to fail. "I will never lose my temper" is an unrealistic goal. "I will apologize when I lose my temper" is a realistic goal.

❺ Ranking Our Priorities[1]

Objective:
Using the ABC technique, the group members will rank their long-term and short-term goals in order of priority and begin making specific plans for accomplishing their major goals (5-20 minutes).

Tell the group that, in addition to the priority questions, there is another effective way of sorting out priorities. Instead of trying to assign each goal a ranking number, assign it a value of A, B, or C.

Write the following on the chalk or marker board.

A = Must do or very high value
B = Should do or medium value
C = Can do or low value

Allow five minutes for the group to work individually, using the ABC technique to prioritize the long-term goals they set for themselves on "Stepping-Stones" (RS-2D), the resource sheet from the last session. (Have extra copies available for

"The horse is made ready for the day of battle, but the victory rests with the Lord."

anyone who wants to start over or was not in the group last time.)

At the end of five minutes, call time, even if people are not finished. Suggest the following: **If you have a long list of goals, you might break it down by subdividing the A goals into A-a, A-b, and A-c.**

If time allows, after determining the "A" goals, encourage the group members to develop plans for accomplishing them. (If time is short, have the parents do this activity at home.)

Goals and priorities motivate us toward the future, but goals without plans are like a ship without a rudder. You may be moving, but you will have very little control over your direction. Good goals deserve good planning.

Proverbs 21:31 says, "The horse is made ready for the day of battle, but the victory rests with the Lord." That gives us the balance between planning and dependence on God. The Bible tells us to plan and prepare, but we also must realize that the outcome is in God's hands.

Hand out three copies of "A Sample Plan" (RS-3C) to each member of the group. Tell them to select three A-priority long-term goals (one for each sheet) and work through the plans for testing and fulfilling those goals. Suggest that one of the major goals be a career goal, since that is a major issue for most men and women in mid-life.

Close the session with prayer, asking for God's wisdom as the group members seek His "easy yoke" and "light burden" for their mid-life years.

Notes:

1. Charles Bradshaw, *You and Your Teen* (Elgin, Ill.: David C. Cook Publishing Co., 1985), 20.

Rekindling The Flame

4

Session Aim:
To show why middle years of
marriage can be rocky and
how disaster can be avoided
by bringing new life back into
the relationship.

READ AS
INTRO:

It is increasingly common for both husbands and wives to
abandon their responsibilities and leave home in this mid-
life stage of life. Life-cycle theorists explain that husbands
and wives going through the various adult stages may be
out of sync with each other. The man has passed through the
trying twenties; he has rooted and extended himself in his
thirties; and he is approaching a mid-life crisis in his forties.
Job satisfaction may be waning; his search for tender-
ness and authenticity is mounting.

The woman may have set aside an outside
career to be primarily a homemaker. But now she may
want to take up a new career. Her mood is determina-
tion, and her search is for strength—creating her own
mid-life crisis as she breaks out of the patterns of the
past. Thus, both husband and wife frequently find
themselves at a crossroads, but for such different
reasons that they can't understand each other.
Couples at this stage of family life are sometimes
vulnerable to extramarital affairs as each partner seeks someone who understands his or
her goals. Understanding the mid-life transition can help couples weather the stresses and
rekindle old romantic flames.

—Charles Bradshaw

***U**nderstanding the mid-life transition can rekindle old romantic flames with your spouse.*

Getting Ready

Scriptures:
Psalm 89:40; Job 1:10;
Matthew 5:27, 28;
I Corinthians 10:13; II Timothy
2:22; John 8:3-11.

1. Prepare copies of "Bring Back the Romance" (RS-4A), "Planting Hedges around Your Marriage" (RS-4B), and "Striking the Match" (RS-4C). Cut RS-4C in half as indicated, making just enough copies for the men to have the top half, and the women to have the bottom half.
2. Using sixteen sheets of blank paper, prepare four sets of four signs with the following words written on them with black marker.
   - *Set One:* (a) **Marriage #1** (b) **Marriage #2** (c) **Marriage #3** (d) **Marriage #4**
   - *Set Two:* (a) **The Dream of the 20s** (b) **The Disillusionment of the 30s** (c) **The Discovery of the 40s** (d) **The Depth of the 50s**
   - *Set Three:* (a) **Differences: ACCOMMODATE** (b) **Differences: ELIMINATE** (c) **Differences: APPRECIATE** (d) **Differences: CELEBRATE**
   - *Set Four:* (a) **Conflict: AVOID** (b) **Conflict: ATTACK** (c) **Conflict: ADJUST** (d) **Conflict: ACCEPT**
   (If you have less than twenty people, merge Set One and Set Two into just one set [for a total of twelve signs], e.g., (a) Marriage #1—The Dream of the 20s, (b) Marriage #2—The Disillusionment of the 30s, etc.)
3. Have additional blank paper available.

❶ Are You Vulnerable?

Objective:
To help the group members separate fact from fiction concerning mid-life transitions and discuss the vulnerability of mid-life couples to extramarital affairs (10 minutes).

Ask group members to brainstorm things they've heard about the mid-life stage of marriage. Capture these ideas on a chalk or marker board with a short phrase. Do not discuss each person's contribution or evaluate whether or not it's true—simply toss into the ring the "conventional wisdom" about mid-life.

Pass out copies of "Bring Back the Romance" (RS-4A). Have the group members indicate how much they agree or disagree with each statement by placing an "x" on the scale from one to five. Give the group a few minutes to complete the work.

Ask volunteers to read each question aloud and then have the group discuss whether they agree or disagree with each statement and why. Do the same for each question. Guide the discussion to include the following information:[1]

*W*hen sexual intimacy fades in a marriage, it usually has little to do with physical causes.

1. Men in their forties, as a rule, have less romantic or sexual responses than younger men.

• Though a husband may be less preoccupied with sex and romance than in earlier years, a man in good health should have no problem making love with his wife into his seventies.

• Though frequency of lovemaking may decline with age, a husband of forty, with more understanding of his wife and with more control, can be a more effective lover than he was at twenty.

• When sexual intimacy fades in a marriage, it usually has little to do with physical causes, but rather with low self-image, fatigue, stress at work, unresolved tensions in the marriage, time pressure, drug use, or too much alcohol.

• Fear of losing one's sexual capacity is often the cause of losing it.

2. In our society today, those who experience a mid-life crisis almost certainly face the temptation to have an extramarital affair.

• While it is true that most extramarital affairs occur between the ages of thirty-five to fifty, it is by no means true that the majority of people in mid-life have affairs or that affairs are "normal."

• Even those who do have affairs do not necessarily have them as a result of a mid-life "crisis."

• Men or women who have affairs do not always select younger partners.

• A mid-life crisis can range from interpersonal assessments and goal adjustments to real internal turmoil—but does not automatically mean that a person is vulnerable to an affair.

3. Affairs are usually entered by married persons for physical gratification.

• Women *and* men have affairs *less* for physical gratification than for the loving acceptance, respect, and understanding they think they are no longer getting from their spouse.

• Infidelity is rare among marriages where the spouses nurture intimacy, receive assurances of the other's acceptance, practice honest self-disclosure, and wholeheartedly affirm one another.

4. The odds against divorce get better with each passing year of marriage.

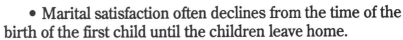

• Marital satisfaction often declines from the time of the birth of the first child until the children leave home.

• Even in the healthiest families, marital pleasures are routinely replaced by parental satisfactions.

• Many twenty-year marriages have a sad profile: few common interests, less expressed affection, general malaise.

• Whereas the "danger zone" for divorce used to be the early years, recent divorce statistics show a second "divorce peak" developing in older marriages.

• Instead of revitalizing their marriage when the children leave home, some spouses are abandoning each other.

• Divorce statistics, however, are created by as many people who don't follow a pattern as by those who do. The goal for Christians is to be part of those who do not follow negative patterns.

❷ Four Marriages in One

Objective:
To help the group members understand that even healthy marriages pass through some difficult stages (15 minutes).

Share the following with the group:

Family therapist and author David Augsburger maintains that marriage is a journey of change and growth. In actuality, couples experience several "marriages within a marriage." Failure to negotiate the passages between the various stages of marriage makes marital dissatisfaction or divorce more likely. As persons change, the marriage changes; but as the marriage is renegotiated at each stage, the persons grow.[2]

Ask for four volunteers to stand and face the group. Pass out the first set of signs which you prepared ahead of time ("Marriage #1," etc.), asking the volunteers to each hold one of the signs about chest high. Then pass out the remaining three sets of signs to various group members. Ask those holding Set Two ("The Dream of the 20s," etc.) to group themselves beside the stage of marriage they think fits their sign. (Skip this step if Set One and Set Two signs have been combined.)

Ask seated group members: **Do these descriptions of the first four decades of married life correspond to your own experience?** (Keep responses brief.)

Then ask those holding Set Three signs (how couples handle "Differences") to group themselves beside the stage of marriage they think applies. Finally, ask those holding Set

*T*here are things we can do to protect our marriages.

Four signs (how couples handle "Conflict") to do the same. (When the smoke clears, all a's should be grouped together, same with b's, c's, d's. See Getting Ready, #2, for designation of the a's, b's, c's, and d's.)

Explain: **According to Augsburger, these four stages of how couples handle "differences" and "conflict" are just aspects of a couple's relationship which change and (hopefully) grow through various phases of a marriage. Other aspects which change and grow include goal-setting, ways of communication, handling feelings, intimacy, roles, and purpose.**

Stimulate a brief discussion by asking the group:

• **As far as handling differences and conflict go, how do Augsburger's different stages compare to your own experience or the experience you have observed in others?**

• **Which transitions were the hardest (between stage 1 and 2? 2 and 3? 3 and 4?) in coping with differences? in managing conflict?**

NOTE to group leader: if the group members want a fuller explanation of what the one-word descriptions mean, provide the following definitions as you have time:[3]

How couples handle DIFFERENCES . . .
- ACCOMMODATE: We tolerate, accommodate, overlook differences to avoid conflict.
- ELIMINATE: We seek to eliminate objectionable differences in our spouse by demanding change.
- APPRECIATE: We discover that differences are creative, necessary parts of us and our marriage.
- CELEBRATE: We delight in our differences and develop them in each other.

How couples manage CONFLICT . . .
- AVOID: We avoid conflict, seeing it as disruptive and destructive of the Dream.
- ATTACK: We explode with frustrated feelings and seek to eliminate differences through fighting, bargaining, pressure.
- ADJUST: We discover fair ways of fighting; we seek mutually satisfactory solutions more quickly.
- ACCEPT: We accept conflict as a healthy process and utilize it to work for mutual growth.

28

P aul doesn't tell us to stand and fight lust as though we can conquer it. He says to flee it!

❸ Planting Hedges

Objective:
To give the group members practical ways to help prevent marital breakdowns (15 minutes).

Knowing that transitions in a marriage can be rough, and that mid-life often adds additional stress, there are things we can do to protect our marriages.

In his book, *Loving Your Marriage Enough to Protect It*, Jerry Jenkins shares several "hedges" he has planted around his own marriage which, he says, are "intended to protect my eyes, my heart, my hands, and therefore my marriage. I direct the rules toward appearances and find that if you take care of how things look, you take care of how they are." Jenkins also admits that most Christian men do not have victory over lust. "Scripture does not imply that we ever shall have victory over lust . . . Rather, Paul instructs Timothy, and thus us, not to conquer or stand and fight, or pray about or resolve, but to *flee* lust."[4]

Distribute copies of "Planting Hedges around Your Marriage" (RS-4B). Divide the group into small teams of men only and women only with three to five per group. Instruct them to:

- *Read* each of the "Hedges" aloud.
- *Discuss*: What effect would it have on my spouse if I planted these hedges around my behavior? What effect would it have on me if my spouse planted these hedges around his/her behavior?
- *Look up and read aloud* the Scriptures at the bottom of the resource sheet.
- *Discuss*: How does each of these Scriptures apply to the stresses I experience in my marriage at this time?

❹ Bring the Romance Back

Objective:
To give the group members ideas for bringing the romance back into the mid-life marriage (5-20 minutes).

While the parents are still in groups of men only and women only, conclude the session as follows:

Besides planting hedges around our marriages, most couples need to invest in renewing the romance that has gotten lost in the whirlwind of parenting and job demands. At least five things are required if romance is going to grow and bloom in a mid-life marriage.

Write the following key words on the chalk or marker board: TIME, COMMITMENT, ACCEPTANCE, SUPPORT, NEWNESS. Define these key words as follows:

- Making TIME for the relationship.
- A COMMITMENT to the person your spouse has become at this stage of life.

Besides planting hedges around our marriages, most of us need to invest in renewing the romance.

- Realistic ACCEPTANCE of who your spouse is, not who you'd like him/her to be.
- Giving SUPPORT to help carry your spouse's burdens.
- Injecting NEWNESS of life into the relationship.

If you are out of time, close the session at this point and pass out copies of "Striking the Match" (RS-4C) which have been cut in half for men and women. But if time allows, after displaying the five key ingredients for renewing romance, rearrange the small groups *(if necessary)* so that you have at least five groups of two or more (still men only and women only). Pass out a blank sheet of paper to each small group and assign one of the key words to each group (TIME, COMMIT-MENT, ACCEPTANCE, SUPPORT, NEWNESS). Instruct the small groups to brainstorm ideas for *striking the match* in a mid-life marriage to reflect their assigned key ingredient. Each group should select a person to record the ideas; allow about five minutes for this exercise.

With the remaining time, invite each small group to share their key word and the ideas with the whole group.

Pass out "Striking the Match" (RS-4C), which has been cut in half. Give the top half to the men and the bottom half to the women. Instruct the group members to write the five key words on the board on the back of their half sheet. As the group members read over the ideas specifically for husbands/ wives (at home, if you are out of time), encourage them to write the key word which applies beside each idea and begin to put them into practice.

Close the session by praying that God will help renew the romance in each of the marriages represented in the group.

NOTE: If you have a full hour, the next session suggests inviting some guests. See point 4 in the Getting Ready section of Session 5 so you can prepare in advance.

Notes:

1. Charles Bradshaw, *You and Your Teen* (Elgin, Ill.: David C. Cook Publishing Co., 1985), 22, 23.

2. David Augsburger, *Sustaining Love: Healing & Growth in the Passages of Marriage* (Ventura, Calif.: Regal Books, 1988), paraphrased, 13, 14.

3. Ibid., 24-25.

4. Jerry Jenkins, *Loving Your Marriage Enough to Protect It* (Chicago: Moody Press, 1993), 2.

All for One and One for All

5

Session Aim:
To determine ways to create a positive family climate through mutual support and decisive living.

Today parents have fierce competition for the influence of young people. However, what's happening in society at large does not necessarily represent each teenager or each family. Parents must take an active role in developing a positive family climate that will help combat the negative trends in society.

Parents can increase their role in teens' character development by being aware of the pressures young people face, how teenagers reason, and what influences them. Values do not develop in a vacuum. Moral development is part of the overall process of growth. Parents should be especially aware of the needs teenagers have which, if unfulfilled at home, will be met elsewhere.

This is especially true for teenagers where the influence of the peer group is strong. Parents cannot always control who their teenagers pick as friends, but they can determine the relationships and climate at home—which in turn can help teens navigate the influences coming from other sources.

Two of the most basic ingredients of a positive family climate are mutual support for one another and being intentional about building family life. Today's session will encourage parents in these areas.

—Charles Bradshaw

One's family doesn't have to duplicate the Brady Bunch to have a positive family climate.

Advance Preparation

Scriptures:
Psalm 133:1; Proverbs 15:17; Proverbs 17:1; Proverbs 17:22.

1. Make photocopies of "An Asset Checklist for Parents and Teens" (RS-5A) and "Patterns of a Strong Family" (RS-5B). (Make extra copies of the "Asset Checklist" for parents of more than one teenager or who wish to take the checklist home to their teens.)
2. Have sheets of blank paper available.
3. Write the Scripture passages for this session on the chalk or marker board.
4. If you have an hour for your session, invite three older parents to attend this session to share during Step 3 what they have done to help create a positive family climate. You might include the pastor or another church leader, parents (possibly a single parent) whose children are now beyond the teen years, grandparents, etc. Try to ask at least one father and one mother (from two different families). Instruct them to take no more than five minutes each.

❶ Not Quite the Brady Bunch

Objective:
To allow parents to review what created a positive family climate in the home of their youth (10 minutes).

If you have invited guests, introduce them and then introduce Unit 2, "Developing a Positive Family Climate," by drawing from the introduction on the preceding page.

One's family doesn't have to duplicate the Brady Bunch or the Cleaver family in order to provide a positive family climate. In fact, even if we came from challenging family backgrounds, there were undoubtedly times when we enjoyed a positive family climate.

Share a memory of something from your own childhood which created a positive family experience—maybe a camping trip, working together, maybe even a crisis that drew you together.

Then invite other group members to contribute their own memories of experiencing a positive family climate. Also include some reports which grew out of negative circumstances.

❷ Add Up the Assets!

Objective:
To help parents identify the assets their teenagers already possess (10 minutes).

One of the major functions of parents is to be a role model. The behavior and beliefs modeled at home are important. Parents also determine the family environment, the context in which teens develop receptivity to parental influence. These become part of the external and internal assets which help young people navigate the challenging teen years.

One sign of a healthy environment is mutual respect and support for individual family members.

Pass out copies of the resource sheet, "An Asset Checklist for Teens and Parents" (RS-5A). Introduce the activity as follows:

Though we may feel overwhelmed at times trying to combat the onslaught of social and cultural pressures which seem to work against our religious and family values, let's check on the assets our teens already possess. This exercise may also show us areas which need strengthening in our relationship with our teens and in the family climate.

Allow four to five minutes for parents to work individually. Spouses may then want to briefly compare how they've each filled out the checklist. (Make available additional copies of "The Asset Checklist" for those who have more than one teenager or would like to have their teenager[s] fill it out. The differences and similarities between parents' and teens' viewpoint could be the basis for a good family discussion.)

❸ A Positive Family Climate

Objective:
To explore how the Bible describes a positive family climate and learn five characteristics of strong families (10-25 minutes).

Draw the group members' attention to the references on the chalk or marker board and ask for volunteers to look up and read each verse aloud. Have the group identify the qualities of a positive family climate as you write the descriptive word or phrase on the board.

Psalm 133:1—(unity)
Proverbs 15:17—(love)
Proverbs 17:1—(peace and quiet)
Proverbs 17:22—(cheerfulness)

Pass out the resource sheet, "Patterns of a Strong Family" (RS-5B). **In addition to the preceding qualities of positive family climate, a research team from Oklahoma State University made an in-depth study of ninety-nine strong Oklahoma families in an attempt to find out what made these families work, what enabled them to experience unity, love, peace, and cheerfulness. Five patterns from these strong families began to emerge very early in the study.**

Have the parents silently read through the description of the five characteristics, tell them to circle each pattern they are following currently in their own family. Then tell them to put a plus (+) beside the one (or two) they are doing the best,

*D*ecisive living means families taking charge of their lives and making things happen.

and a minus (-) beside the one (or two) they most need to work on as a family.

If you have a full hour for your session, use about fifteen minutes at this point to hear from the guest parents who have created a positive family climate in their homes. These sharings should be brief (about five minutes each).

❹ Mutual Support/ Decisive Living

Objective:
To help the group members discover practical ways to develop a positive family climate through mutual support and decisive living (10 minutes).

Explain that Charles Bradshaw summarizes these patterns of strong families into two main concepts: mutual support and decisive living.[1] Define each of these concepts as follows:

MUTUAL SUPPORT: One of the signs of a healthy environment for moral development is mutual respect and support for individual family members. The child respects the adults in his or her world, but the adult must also communicate respect for the child, his or her feelings, perspectives, and interests. Teens need to feel they are important. The families in this study took an active interest in the activities of each member.

Ask the group for specific examples of mutual support they experienced in their family of origin or have witnessed in other families they admire. Keep these sharings brief, allowing two to three minutes. Then continue:

DECISIVE LIVING: Strong family ties do not leap into existence by themselves; they are built intentionally. Decisive living means that families take charge of their lives and make things happen. Too many families drift along and are subject to whatever happens—good, bad, or indifferent. If we want to experience a family environment that's good for all members, we need to make it happen!

Ask group members to suggest questions parents could ask to help themselves become more intentional in their family life. Guide the discussion to include the following:

*   What are we currently missing in the life of our family that would enrich us?
*   What are we missing that we will later regret?
*   Are either father or mother absent too often from the family?
*   What individual activities could we curtail in order to have more time together?

- What kinds of activities could bring us together in a natural way?

Now ask group members to suggest some of the traps which work against a positive family climate. Their ideas may include some of the following:

- Busyness. (The inattentiveness of busy parents is the factor most often cited as contributing to behavior problems in children.)
- The amount of time spent watching television.
- Unresolved conflict between parents and teens.
- Tension in the marriage.
- Lack of support for single-parent or blended families.

After this introduction to the concepts of mutual support and decisive living, divide the group into small groups of four to six persons. Again, spouses should be in different groups to give greater diversity of sharing and ideas in each group. Encourage each group to share among themselves, answering the following questions:

1. **What practical ways of mutual support have we worked on or experienced in our family?**
2. **What practical ways of decisive living have we worked on or experienced in our family?**

Suggest that the group members take notes on these ideas on the bottom of their resource sheet, "Patterns of a Strong Family" (RS-5B), in the sections marked "Mutual Support" and "Decisive Living."

---

❺ Taking It Home

Objective:
To give an opportunity for parents to decide one thing they are going to do in the coming week to take charge of their family climate (5 minutes).

In the remaining minutes of the session, encourage spouses to get together and decide *one thing* they are going to work on to develop more mutual support among family members and *one way* to take charge of their family climate (decisive living). Single parents, or those with no partner present, should get together with one other person and share their plans with each other. Encourage all "pairs" to pray together about their decision before leaving.

Notes:

1. Charles Bradshaw, *You and Your Teen* (Elgin, Ill.: David C. Cook Publishing Co., 1985), 30, 31.

Ending the Shootouts

6

Session Aim:
To help parents identify and effectively deal with any conflicts due to value differences between themselves and their teens.

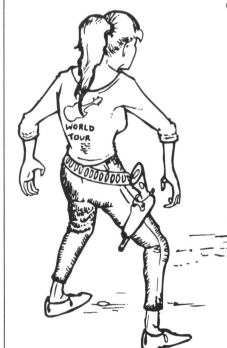

Teenagers are discovering who they are and what they think and believe. Often, they reject concepts they once accepted simply because they were told those things by family, teachers, or other adults. The ideas are not yet theirs; they have not yet "personalized" them.

In the process of reexamination, teens accept or reject everything from values and standards to styles and politics. Usually, personalizing is a gradual process with a manageable degree of tension. However, it can be marked by alienation, hostility, and rebellion. Personality, environment, and parental style all seem to influence how internalization takes place, and most parents wish they knew the secret formula for navigating it with peace and reason.

Every home has a certain amount of conflict. It's a fact of life. In the home, the issues may range from participating in family activities, curfew and dating, taking a job after school, smoking or drinking, to styles of clothes or hair. For the adolescent, most conflict revolves around the developmental task of establishing independence.

Parents need to keep in mind that conflict itself is not necessarily the problem, but rather how conflicts are handled.

—*Charles Bradshaw*

*E*very home has a certain amount of conflict. It's a fact of life.

Getting Ready

Scriptures:
James 4:1; Genesis 4:1-16; Genesis 13:5-12; I Samuel 24:1-13; Acts 15:1-29, 36-41; I Peter 3:8, 9; Proverbs 15:1.

1. Make photocopies of the resource sheets, "The Good, the Bad, and the Ugly" (RS-6A), "Ways to Deal with Conflict" (RS-6B), and "Handling Conflict the ASRAC Way" (RS-6C).

❶ Old Conflicts Never Die

Objective:
To recall how conflict was handled in the parents' youth and how that influenced them (10 minutes).

Distribute copies of "The Good, the Bad, and the Ugly" (RS-6A), then tell the group members to get comfortable, close their eyes, and think back to their own adolescence. Set the mood for a time of reflection:

Remember when you were a teenager—between twelve and eighteen years old . . . Walk into the junior high or high school you attended . . . Stop and talk with your friends . . . What was important to you as an adolescent? . . . How important were your friends? . . . family? . . . church?

Allow a few moments for the group members to recall their teenage years. Then proceed.

Now imagine returning home—it could be after school or later in the evening. Suddenly, you are into a major conflict with your mother or father or both. It might have been over anything—something you failed to do, your appearance, getting in late, your choice of friends, etc. Relive it for a moment, remembering all the details you can.

After group members have recalled an incident from their youth, instruct them to answer the questions on the resource sheet. When they finish, ask for three volunteers to describe the conflict they remember from their youth. After each person shares, ask these question:

*   **What was your parents' real goal?** (Don't settle for the surface dispute over hair, clothes, or curfew. Encourage them to imagine their parents deeper motives and objectives.)
*   **What was your real goal?** (Again, don't settle for surface issues.)
*   **What did you learn about conflict from your experience as an adolescent?** (Question 5.)

Withdrawing from conflict reflects low concern for achieving needs or preserving relationships.

❷ Ways To Deal With Conflict

Objective:
To discover desirable ways of dealing with conflict by examining examples of five common responses (10 minutes).

Divide the group into five teams and assign each team one of the following Scripture passages to study to discover what style (a one-word label) was used in dealing with conflict. Ask each team to designate a reporter to describe its findings to the whole group. At this point, do not insist on the specific words in parentheses.

1. *Genesis 4:1-16*—(win)
2. *Genesis 13:5-12*—(compromise)
3. *I Samuel 24:1-13*—(yield)
4. *Acts 15:1-29*—(resolve)
5. *Acts 15:36-41*—(withdraw)

Reconvene the whole group and ask for the reports. Invite each representative to briefly describe the conflict and the style used in dealing with it.

Explain that James Fairfield, in his book, *When You Don't Agree*, suggests that there are five common styles people use in dealing with conflict.[1] As you name and describe each one, ask the group to figure out which biblical incident most fits that style.

1. Withdraw. This is the tendency to view conflict as so unpleasant and unresolvable that it is better to separate—physically or psychologically. (Acts 15:36-41, Paul and Barnabas separate.)

2. Win. When you think your well-being, your interests, or your self-concept is threatened, you may choose to go all out to win, being willing to sacrifice the relationship in the process. (Genesis 4:1-16, Cain kills Abel).

3. Yield. "Give in to get along" describes this style. You may not like it, but it is a way to end the conflict. (I Samuel 24:1-13, David pledges allegiance to Saul.)

4. Compromise. With this you may concede some of your demands but only when you are assured of obtaining others. (Genesis 13:5-12, Abraham and Lot divide the grazing lands of Canaan.)

5. Resolve. Through open and direct communication, a solution is achieved that attempts to satisfy all parties. This may or may not include what everyone wants, but rather what everyone agrees is best. (Acts 15:1-29, the church agrees not to require circumcision of Gentile believers.)

Winning meets your needs but may sacrifice the relationship.

❸ Which Way Is Best?

Objective:
To help the parents discover the implications of using the various styles of conflict resolution (5 minutes).

Pass out copies of "Ways to Deal with Conflict" (RS-6B), and communicate the following evaluation:

You may be asking, "Which style is best?" Except for resolving a conflict, which isn't always possible, no other style is universally best, but this diagram shows some trade-offs in achieving goals or maintaining the relationship.

As you can see from the diagram, *Yield* maintains the relationship but sacrifices the goals. In the long run, however, too frequent yielding can damage the relationship because it destroys respect.

***Resolve* is the most desirable style because it strengthens relationships as you seek to meet personal needs.**

***Win* may achieve a goal but can sacrifice the relationship. In a family, personal relationships should be more important than any goal other than direct obedience to God.**

***Withdraw* has the lowest value because the person gives up both achieving goals and fostering the relationship. However, if this style is used only temporarily as a cooling-off step, it can be beneficial.**

***Compromise* attempts to work out some needs, but the bargaining involved may mean that you compromise some of your goals.**

Draw the groups' attention to the bottom of the page where three ways of "winning" are described. Ask a couple of volunteers to describe how their parents used one of those ways to "win" in the conflict example they identified on the first resource sheet (RS-6A) at the beginning of this session. **How did this make you feel? Are there times when "winning" is essential?** Allow several minutes to discuss this.

❹ The ASRAC Method[2]

Objective:
To learn a method of conflict resolution and gain skill in its use through roleplays (20-35 minutes).

Distribute copies of "Handling Conflict the ASRAC Way" (RS-6C). Ask two volunteers to read the two verses at the top of this sheet, I Peter 3:8, 9 and Proverbs 15:1.

These verses indicate that Christians—and Christian parents in particular—are called to be healers. It is not our role to win, but to heal. That does not mean giving in all the time. It means taking steps to protect and

Compromising may achieve some of your needs while sacrificing others.

build the relationship while finding mutually acceptable goals.

Discuss the five steps of the ASRAC method, making sure the group members understand all five steps.

Now ask the parents to briefly describe three or four conflict situations that recently have arisen between themselves and their teenagers. Do not let the parents tell how they handled the conflict or give blow-by-blow descriptions of any "fights" that ensued. All they should describe is the facts surrounding the situation and the goals or the positions held by the parent and teen.

Select one of the situations that seems typical and is not too complex (a curfew dispute, disagreement over styles, music, homework, etc.), and then invite two volunteers from the group to roleplay the situation, adjusting the gender of the characters in the roleplay according to that of the volunteer team, "girl" for "boy," or "mother" for "father," etc.

Have the "teenager" and "parent" assume their respective roles with the parent trying to practice the ASRAC way of handling the conflict. (You can add a second parent if it seems desirable.) Give the team about five minutes to resolve the conflict. When the roleplay is completed, lead the group in discussing the following questions:

1. **In what ways did the parent show ACCEPTANCE of the teenager's resentment or fear?**
2. **How did the parent SHARE concern with the teenager?**
3. **What did the parent do to REFLECT the emotions of the teenager?**
4. **How did the parent ADVOCATE a resolution/solution that would end the conflict?**
5. **How did the parent CONFIRM the end of the conflict?**

If you have time, divide the group into separate roleplay teams of three people each, one to be a parent, one to be a teen, and the third to observe the interaction. Have the teams select one of the conflict situations suggested earlier by the whole group and roleplay an attempt to resolve the conflict. After a few minutes, they should evaluate the effort according to the ASRAC method.

Resolving the conflict strengthens the relationship while meeting personal needs.

Encourage the team members to change roles and repeat the exercise as time allows.

Notes:

1. James G. T. Fairchild, *When You Don't Agree: A Guide to Resolving Marriage and Family Conflicts* (Scottdale, Penn.: Herald Press, 1977), 19.
2. Charles Bradshaw, *You and Your Teen* (Elgin, Ill.: David C. Cook Publishing Co., 1985), 34.

Doin' the Right Thing

7

Session Aim:
To help parents understand the basis for moral decisions and how they can help their teens make right choices.

FERD

Westion is

We once assumed that most children—if raised in a godly home—would make it through adolescence unscathed. We took comfort in Proverbs 22:6: "Train a child in the way he should go, and when he is old he will not turn from it" . . . thinking that "old" must surely mean no more than eighteen or twenty.

Then a police car rolls up in front of our house—with our son in it. Or our daughter announces that she just had an abortion. Or our son declares he is gay.

Casualties were always someone else's kids. Now they're ours . . . or so close to home that we no longer feel safe.

What did we do wrong?

Maybe nothing. If our perfect Heavenly Father can have disobedient children, we know that loving care does not always "succeed" in producing righteous children. And yet we care too much not to try. Furthermore, we can be encouraged by a 1990 study of sixth to twelfth graders showing that youth who attend religious services at least once or twice a month are nearly half as likely to engage in "at-risk" behaviors (such as frequent alcohol use, problem drug use, sexual activity, attempted suicide) as those who rarely or never attend church.[1] (see pg 48)

So, what can we do to encourage growth in our teen's moral behavior?

Youth who attend religious services are only half as likely to engage in "at-risk" behaviors.

Getting Ready

Scriptures:
James 4:17; Luke 12:48b;
Romans 1:18; Matthew 11:29;
John 14:15; I John 4:19.

1. Prepare copies of "Top Influences on Teens" (RS-7A), "Moral Behavior" (RS-7B), and "In the Thick of It" (RS-7C). For the last resource sheet, make an *extra* copy for each four group members. For instance, if you have a group of twenty people, you would need a total of twenty-five copies.

❶ A Different World?

Objective:
To examine the comparative influences on teens and to help parents consider how life has changed since they were young (10 minutes).

Begin the session by distributing copies of "Top Influences on Teens" (RS-7A). Explain that teenagers were surveyed in 1960 and again in 1980 concerning what influenced their values and behaviors most. In 1960, the parents had the greatest impact on the teenagers, but in 1980, friends and peers moved up to the number one spot.

Ask the group members to notice that in the lightly shaded area below each set of 1960 and 1980 bars on the chart there is space for a 1990 bar. Ask them to make a mark on the chart where they think the 1990 bar would reach for each category. Go over each category, discussing their estimates and rationale.

Then provide the following new information: **In 1990, Junior Achievement contracted with the Gallup Organization to examine the attitudes of American students in a number of areas. While the research does not correspond directly to the research we have just examined, we can make some general comparisons. For instance, the following percentage of American youth rated these persons to be "very important" as role models:[2]**

Parents—91 percent.
Friends—69 percent.
Teachers—50 percent.
Religious leaders—41 percent.
Successful athletes (popular heroes)—25 percent.

Even though the research question dealt with "role models" rather than "top influences on teens," it is significant that 91 percent of young people consider parents "very important."

Now invite the group to identify some significant differences in what their teens face compared to past generations. You might want to emphasize the following points:

Giving kids increased freedom is different than withdrawing from them emotionally.

- **Less extended-family support.** Grandpa and grandma aren't around to throw an arm around the kids when they need it.
- **Kids are no longer "needed,"** as they once were, on the farm or in the family business. Even in terms of faith, Dr. Robert Laurent claims that the number one reason teens reject religion is that they cannot find meaningful involvement in the church.[3]
- **Teens must make major choices at earlier ages.** Long before they are ready, teens feel they must decide what they want to be to get a jump on training. In moral areas, the need to decide about drugs, sex, alcohol—and in some cases whether to carry a weapon for protection—comes earlier and earlier.
- **Parents back off too much.** Launching or releasing our kids is an important process, but giving kids increased freedom is different from withdrawing from them emotionally.
- **Power of the media.** When today's parents were young, the electronic media was less sophisticated in its power of persuasion. Now, it is almost irresistible.

As tempting as it is to want to reproduce the past, growing up was never easy. For instance, Peter the Hermit, the fiery monk who spearheaded the first crusade in A.D. 1095, said this:

> **Young people today think of nothing but themselves; they have no reverence for parents or old age, they are impatient of all restraint, they talk as if they knew everything. What passes for wisdom with us is foolishness to them. As for the girls, they are forward, immodest, and unwomanly in speech, behavior and dress.**

Sound familiar? But we will help our young people most if, instead of complaining about them, we give them better tools for making moral decisions.

❷ The Components of Moral Behavior

Objective:
To help the parents discover a model for understanding how moral behavior develops (10 minutes).

Distribute copies of "Moral Behavior" (RS-7B) and divide the group into teams of four people each. Suggest that two people in the group silently read the column titled, "Knowledge," while the other two silently read the column titled, "Will." Then have each pair explain what they've read to the other pair so everyone has a full understanding of how knowledge and will interact in producing moral behavior.

You may want to walk around to the groups to aid discussion and answer questions.

❸ Adjusting As Kids Get Older

Objective:
To help the parents understand how their role in relation to moral training must change as a child matures (10 minutes).

While the teams are studying the model in the exercise above, write on your chalk or marker board the appropriate subtitles (in boldface, below) under the heading KNOWLEDGE on the left and under WILL on the right.

Reconvene the large group and ask parents how they think their role might change for each component as their child moves through adolescence into adulthood. Add your input based on the following information only where the group's ideas are weak.

KNOWLEDGE

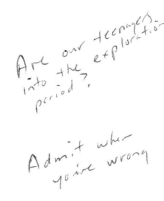

1. Experience and exploration is as enticing to teens as to a four-year-old. But the challenge may change from a tree to climb to experimenting with drugs. The wise parent of a teen will extend trust as much as possible and reserve prohibitions for real danger.

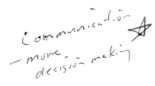

2. Example remains a vital role for the parent. The teen's increased ability to detect inconsistencies requires the parent to pay close attention to integrity. Repentance and admission of failure are critical to maintaining integrity. If the parent does not expect perfection of the teen, the teen will not demand it of the parent, but the teen will expect honesty and humility.

3. Revelation will be less effective in influencing older children if it is based on the raw authority of the parent. But dialogue gains an increasingly valuable place. A teen should know that he or she can sometimes change his parents' opinions. If there's a chance of that, there is reason to talk.

Our task at this stage includes accomplishing the process of releasing our children.

WILL

1. Consequences. During the teen years, the parents' role should change from being the "manager of consequences" to the "maintainer of limits." By adulthood, even that should give way to brotherly care and concern. The parental role must change more in this element than in any other.

2. Attitudes. The parents' role here stays relatively the same. Attitudes are responses of the heart; we can never require their existence within another person. We can only nurture them through example and affirmation.

3. Grace. Just as we discovered that we can love God, others, and what is good because He first loved us, so our children and teens can love more as we love them. In this area, our input can be ongoing, steady.

Because God loves us!

Summarize the discussion: **Many of us struggle with how much influence peers have on our teens. It may be helpful to understand peer influence in terms of "consequences." Approval or disapproval is a form of rewards and punishments. And real rejection would be as painful for us as for our teenagers.**

This understanding may help us empathize with them. In a very proper way, they are transferring their focus from parents to a larger world. In the meantime, we can continue to influence them by assuring them that we will never reject them and by affirming them whenever possible. We should do our part to keep the home the most secure, most affirming place in our teen's life. Avoid letting your teenager get so discouraged that he or she thinks there is no way to win at home. This may be the primary meaning of the warning in Ephesians 6:4a— "Fathers, do not exasperate your children."

Our task

Finally, we must remember that our task at this stage includes accomplishing the process of releasing our children. James Dobson points out that doing everything right will not guarantee perfect children. "God, the perfect Father, lost Adam and Eve in that they both went into sin. If it were possible to prevent willful defiance, He certainly should have been able to do it. But they had free choice, and even God would not take it from them, nor can I take it from my children."[4]

The example of the parents' love for, and faithfulness to, each other can be a powerful influence on the teen.

❹ Trial and Error

Objective:
To help the parents evaluate their role in seeking a solution to the moral dilemmas they may face with their teenagers (15-30 minutes).

Divide the group into teams of four people each, and then ask each group to select a moderator. Give the moderators five copies of "In the Thick of It" (RS-7C). Instruct the moderators that they are not to let their team members see the sheets. Instead, moderators should fold and then tear one sheet along the dotted lines and give the respective "roles" of "father," "mother," and "teenager" to the other members of the small group.

Now, instruct everyone that the small groups will have five minutes to do their roleplays among themselves. Those people playing the parental roles should try to remember the elements of moral behavior and the ways parents can best influence teens as they work on the problem.

When five minutes have passed, call time. The moderators should then pass out the remaining copies of "In the Thick of It" (RS-7C), and lead their small groups in discussing the questions at the bottom of the sheet.

If people wish to discuss their answers, you might suggest the following: (1—Experience will provide knowledge but at a high price. 2—Observing the example of the parents' love for, and faithfulness to, each other can be a powerful influence on the teen. 3—Instruction that is factually and biblically based has the most advantage for influence. Exaggeration and guilt trips will do little lasting good. 4—Consequences concerning privileges might be related to safe behavior [abstinence]; for instance, the teen that does not value his or her virginity might not be mature enough drive a car. 5—Example and affirmation are some of the most effective influences in the teen years.)

If you have time, reconvene the large group and have the parents use the back of "In the Thick of It" (RS-7C) to write out a statement of their aspirations for their teens. To get them started, write the following statement on the chalk or marker board: **"In terms of moral behavior, when my children come to the end of their teen years, I want them to . . ."** and have them copy it, completing their statement of aspirations.

Allow several minutes for the parents to complete their statements, then divide the group into pairs (husbands and wives together, where possible) and encourage them to go over their expectations, evaluating and revising them according to the questions on the other side of the resource sheet. Encourage couples to select the three top priorities they can

Example and affirmation are some of the most effective influences in the teen years.

agree on, and decide how they will work toward helping their teen realize those expectations.

Close the session in prayer, asking God to guard the parents from exasperating their teens, and to guide them in raising their teens in the training and instruction of the Lord. (See Eph. 6:4.)

Notes:

1. "The Faith Factor," *Source*, Vol. VII, No. 1, February 1992, 1. Based on a Search Institute's study of eighteen at-risk behaviors among 47,000 public school students.

2. Richard D. Van Scotter and Peter J. Harder, "International Youth Survey: The United States and Japan," a paper based on the Analytic Report produced by the Gallup Organization, Princeton, N. J., for Junior Achievement, Inc., 1990.

3. Robert Laurent, *Keeping Your Teen in Touch with God* (Elgin, Ill.: David C. Cook Publishing Co., 1988), 21.

4. James Dobson, "Answers to a Parent's Sigh: An Interview with James Dobson," *Moody Monthly*, Feb. 1984.

Growing Confident Teens

8

Session Aim:
To acquaint parents with the developmental tasks of teenagers and to inform them how to help teens accomplish these tasks.

A dolescence means "the period of growth to maturity." During this time the young person changes physically, sexually, emotionally, intellectually, and socially. The changes sometimes come quickly, and immature young people do not always adjust efficiently. This has led many people to conclude that adolescence is a disruptive period of rebellion and turmoil.

In spite of the rapid growth and changes during this time, adolescents in general are not immune to parental values. Though all adolescents have major tasks to accomplish as a prerequisite to further development, how these tasks are accomplished will largely relate to the value systems of their nuclear family.

They must first adjust to physical changes, second to influences of great social pressures, and third to the challenge of making life-determining decisions about values, beliefs, identity, careers, and their relationship with others, including the opposite sex.

The parental task is learning how to let go. Ultimately, parenthood is a process of working oneself out of a job. This doesn't happen overnight. We must prepare our teens for launching by equipping them to take more and more responsibility for their lives and their decisions.

—*Charles Bradshaw*

I n spite of peer pressure, adolescents are not immune to parental values.

Getting Ready

Scriptures:
I Corinthians 13:11; Ephesians 4:14, 15; Luke 15:11-32; verses from II Samuel 11, 13—15, 18

1. Prepare one photocopy of "Adolescence Is . . ." (RS-8A) and cut apart the five definitions. Put each one in a separate envelope.
2. Prepare photocopies of "Developmental Tasks of Teenagers" (RS-8B), "Three Parents" (RS-8C), and "General Guidelines for Letting Go" (RS-8D) for all the group members.

❶ It's Not Easy Being a Teenager!

Objective:
To help parents affirm their essential task—preparing teens to leave home—by exploring the five developmental tasks of teenagers (15 minutes).

As the parents arrive, pass out the five sealed envelopes containing the "definitions" of adolescence from "Adolescence Is . . ." (RS-8A) to five different group members. Tell them to hold on to the envelope until asked to share its contents.

Ask the group: **What is an adolescent?** Encourage the group members to give you about ten brief descriptive words or phrases—serious or otherwise! (You might list these on the chalk or marker board.) Then say:

Everyone has an opinion about adolescence. Here are a few more. Ask those with the envelopes to open them and each read the "definition" enclosed.

After everyone has had a good laugh, introduce Unit III by summarizing the information in the introduction on the preceding page. Especially note the last two paragraphs: even though the teen years can be turbulent and perplexing to parents, something important is happening during this time. Both teenagers and their parents have important tasks to accomplish.

Ask two volunteers to look up and read aloud I Corinthians 13:11 and Ephesians 4:14, 15.

Scripture encourages all of us to "grow up" spiritually, to become more mature. Obviously, it's a process; we don't become spiritually mature overnight. This is helpful to remember with our teenagers. We want them to act maturely; yet sometimes we still treat them like children. Preparing our teens for launching is a process for both parents and teens.

Your teenagers will try to tell you that you don't know anything. (Sound familiar?) This is the time when the peer group becomes increasingly important. But peers cannot help your teenager complete his or her developmental tasks. In fact, the word *peers* means

Young people are incapable of informing themselves of all they need to know to become mature adults.

"those at the same level of insight, awareness, and maturity." By definition, young people are incapable of informing themselves of all they need to know to become mature adults.[1] (Of course, it doesn't do any good to tell them that—but it's nice to know parents and other significant adults have an important role, in spite of what your teenager says!)

Distribute copies of "Developmental Tasks of Teenagers" (RS-8B). Then share the following:

In our first session, we noted that the developmental tasks of teenagers are similar to those of the mid-life adult. Let's take a closer look at how these developmental tasks relate to the adolescent.

One by one, ask different group members to read the five developmental tasks aloud. After each task is read, you might ask one or more of the following:

1. How did you feel about these changes when you were a teen? What feelings does your own teen have about this task?
2. What were the problems and difficulties you faced in accomplishing this task when you were a teenager? What problems and difficulties does your own teen face?

Do not get into a major discussion on any one point, however. Group feedback is simply to help the group members identify with the reality of these tasks.

❷ Parenting Patterns

Objective:
To compare the parenting patterns of the father of the Prodigal Son and King David (20 minutes).

Distribute copies of "Three Parents" (RS-8C), then ask parents to group themselves into six smaller teams of two or more persons. Introduce the Bible study by saying:

The biblical story of the Prodigal Son demonstrates the process of working through the developmental tasks within the family. And it wasn't particularly easy for the parent.

Instruct the group members to turn to and read Luke 15:11-24. Working together, small group members should briefly fill out each section of the column for this story. At the end of five minutes, ask each team to share its answers for one of the points until all six have been covered. Their answers should be similar to the following:

The parents of the Prodigal Son didn't have it particularly easy, but they made it.

Father—Prodigal
(Luke 15:11-32)

(1. Foolish decision; pride; greed; immaturity.

2. Willing to "let go"; gave responsibility; let son make mistakes; did not protect from consequences.

3. Did not intervene or rescue; was patient; still loved his son.

4. Took the initiative [watched for and ran to his son]; affectionate; threw his arms around him.

5. Compassion; forgiveness; unconditional love.

6. Celebration; son repentant; son had "come to his senses"; parent-son relationship restored.)

While the group members are still in the small groups, direct their attention to the second biblical parent:

We also have a poor example of a parent in Scripture. King David was one of the great men in the Old Testament. We know him for his deep confidence in God, a man after God's own heart. Unfortunately, however, from the life of David we can discover ways in which a parent can undermine the young person's developmental tasks.

Assign each of the "teams" only one section on the resource sheet for the second story—e.g., team #1 works on section 1, team #2 works on section 2, etc. If you have more than six groups, assign two groups to work on section 1, etc. Allow five minutes for small group work (or less, if all seem finished). Ask team #1 to share their discoveries with the larger group. As each team shares the results of its study, the other group members may wish to fill in the rest of the sections in the King David column. Possible answers for each section include:

King David—Absalom
(II Samuel 11, 13—15, 18)

(1. Poor example of father; similar problems in sons—sexual immorality, murder; unresolved family problems; sibling hatred which led to murder.

2. Anger; no parental correction; no restoration.

3. Constant mourning; fear; still loved his son.

4. Unexpressed affection; finally kissed his son [too late?].

5. Incomplete forgiveness; would not see son for two years; message of rejection.

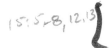

U nfortunately, David's life demonstrates how a parent can undermine a young person's developmental tasks.

(15:5-8, 12, 13)

6. Son became bitter; conspired against father; son's untimely death; relationship never restored; father's regret.)

If time permits, ask for comments or comparisons between the two biblical parents from the group members.

❸ Bringing It Home

Objective:
To help parents compare their own parenting to the two biblical fathers and choose one area that needs work in the coming week (10-25 minutes).

Encourage the group members to think prayerfully how the example of the two Biblical parents applies to their own parenting. Call attention to the third column on "Three Parents" (RS-8C), and encourage the group members to think of one specific problem or developmental task that is a particular challenge at this stage in their teen's life. Instruct them to fill out the column labeled "Me—My Teen," as each section applies to their own situation. Suggest that some sections might be filled out as a prayer, asking God for help in that area and the desired positive response. Allow at least five minutes for individual reflection and writing.

Pass out copies of "General Guidelines of Letting Go" (RS-8D) for parents to take home. Or, if time allows, you might use this resource in one of the following ways:

Option 1. Ask different volunteers to read each of the "Guidelines" for letting go aloud to the group. Generate a discussion among group members as to which of these "Guidelines" is the most challenging to them personally. Why? What are the special challenges for single parents? for blended families?

Option 2. Working in pairs (as couples where this is possible), have group members read the "Guidelines" together, then identify one or two which are the most challenging in their own parenting. Encourage partners to brainstorm specific ways they could apply this rule at home in the coming week.

Option 3. After reading through all the "Guidelines" for letting go, have each person choose a partner (spouse or otherwise). Instruct each pair to think of a typical dialog interaction between a parent and teen, first to express a negative application of one of the guidelines, then a positive application of the same guideline. Humor is okay! Allow several minutes for partners to prepare, then ask for different pairs to share their short dialog interactions with the whole group.

*W*e must prepare our teens for launching by equipping them to take more and more responsibility for their lives and decisions.

In the last few minutes of the session, encourage the group members to choose a prayer partner and share the following:

- **At least one positive strength I see in the way I relate to my own teenage son or daughter.**
- **One area of weakness/failure I am experiencing in relating to my teenage son or daughter.**

Encourage partners to pray for each other in the area of weakness.

Notes:

1. H. Stephen Glenn and Jane Nelsen, *Raising Self-Reliant Children in a Self-Indulgent World* (New York: St. Martin's Press, 1989), 29.

Freedom and Responsibility

9

Session Aim:
To help parents understand that the major developmental task of teenagers is independence and how this can be accomplished through growth in responsibility.

Ask a question

If any signpost marks the beginning of adulthood, it is the assumption of responsibility. Parents often envy other families in which the teenagers seem more responsible. Teens seem to want responsibility in some areas (like staying out later at night, taking trips on weekends with their friends, or use of the family car) but not others (like buying their own clothes, watching little brother after school, or the upkeep of the yard).

The major developmental task of teenagers is growth toward independence. (We may hate to think of the kids leaving home—until we consider the alternative!) But the key to independence is responsibility. Can responsibility be taught? Is responsibility more caught than taught? Can we set up a climate conducive to "catching" responsibility? What barriers do parents unintentionally erect? Most rebellion is a teen's immature way of saying, "When will you understand that I'm my own person!" Understanding that movement toward autonomy is a positive thing, and balancing the amount of freedom with appropriate responsibility can help parents turn battles into building blocks.

—*Charles Bradshaw*

Sometimes the push-pull between dependence and independence feels like plain old rebellion!

Getting Ready

Scriptures:
Isaiah 1:2; Proverbs 10:19; 15:4; 17:9; 17:27; I Thessalonians 2:11, 12; 5:14

1. Make two photocopies of "Teens vs. Parents" (RS-9A) and cut apart the three sections as indicated. Put the two A sections in an envelope and label it "A," then do the same for sections B and C.
2. Prepare photocopies of "Barriers and Builders" (RS-9B), "Freedoms Earned through Responsibility" (RS-9C), and "Parents Are People, Too" (RS-9D).
3. Write the following Scripture references on the chalk or marker board: Proverbs 10:19; Proverbs 15:4a; Proverbs 17:9; Proverbs 17:27; I Thessalonians 2:11, 12; I Thessalonians 5:14.

❶ On the Road to Autonomy

Objective:
To identify three types of autonomy that teenagers are seeking in their quest for independence (10 minutes).

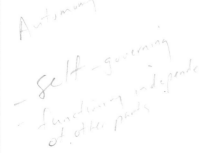

As the group members arrive, pass out the three envelopes you prepared in advance to three couples. Ask each couple to read over the dialog and choose who is going to read which part when called upon.

Introduce the session as follows:

In our last session we talked about the "developmental tasks" of teenagers and the need for parents to "let go" as our teens approach adulthood. It all sounded rational at the time. But what happened when you went home? (Allow a few volunteers to share their experiences.) **Did you have any interactions with your teenagers that sounded something like this?**

Ask the couple with envelope A from "Teens vs. Parents" (RS-9A) to read their dialog for the group.

Frankly, sometimes that push-pull between dependence and independence feels like plain old rebellion! We shouldn't be too surprised, however. In Isaiah 1:2 God said He has the same problem with His people Israel: "For the Lord has spoken: 'I reared children and brought them up, but they have rebelled against me'"!

Now invite the other two couples to read their dialogs. Most parents will be able to identify with at least one of the interactions—if not all three!

The need for adolescents to think and act independently is very real. In fact, Carol Kuykendall, in her book _Learning to Let Go_, points out that teenagers strive for three types of autonomy in their quest for independence.

If we don't let them try out their wings, the message we give is, "You aren't capable."

On the chalkboard, write the following three phrases:
- **BEHAVIORAL AUTONOMY**
- **EMOTIONAL AUTONOMY**
- **VALUE AUTONOMY**

Briefly define the three types of autonomy as follows:[1]

- *Behavioral autonomy* **often results in conflicts about dating, types of activities, choice of friends, curfews, clothes, and money.**
- *Emotional autonomy* **means the transfer of emotional attachment from family members to peers or even other adults in an effort to be more self-reliant and develop more self-control.**
- *Value autonomy* **is a search for self-identity, defining one's own moral and religious values, vocational choices, and life goals.**

Now ask: **Which of these struggles for autonomy did you see at work in the three roleplays we just witnessed?** (Not wanting to be with family; OK to be with someone else's family; challenging the curfew; wanting to skip church or go to a different church.)

Kuykendall says we can either accept and facilitate this separation process in a positive way, or we can thwart our teen's efforts, making the process more traumatic for both parents and teens.[2]

Overhead

quote

---

❷ Barriers and Builders

Objective:
To make parents aware of five barriers to teenagers' self-confidence and five builders of teens' confidence
(15 minutes).

Move into the next activity with the following comments:
Parents have a hard time giving up control because teens often seem so irresponsible. On the other hand, if we don't let them try out their wings, the message we give is, "You aren't capable." To accomplish their developmental tasks in a healthy way, however, teens need to feel, "I'm capable; I'm significant; I'm influential."

Let's look at five parental behaviors that can undermine teenagers' self-confidence and block their growth in responsibility.

Pass out copies of "Barriers and Builders" (RS-9B). Ask a volunteer to read the first Barrier aloud to the group and its corresponding Builder in the right-hand column. Continue with each set of Barriers and Builders.

Some questions might come up regarding Barriers and Builders. For example:

W e must remember that young people don't "arrive" at full maturity all at once.

- *If we're not supposed to be "directing," how are we supposed to train our children to do something correctly?* (There is a time for training; there is also a time to allow for other ways of doing things, and for the teen to take responsibility for how to get something done.)
- *Shouldn't we have high expectations for our teens?* (Yes, but we must also acknowledge that young people don't "arrive" all at once. We can affirm steps of progress toward the goal of excellence without always pointing out the deficiencies. The first encourages; the other discourages.)

Now divide the group into at least five small groups of two to four persons. Assign one set of "Barriers/Builders" to each group. Instruct small groups to select a specific incident from their own interactions with teens which personifies the Barrier they've been assigned. Then they should "rewrite the script" for that incident using the Builder instead, and prepare both interactions as a short roleplay.

Allow five minutes for small groups to prepare. Then ask small groups to present their roleplays, first the interaction using the Barrier, then replaying it using a Builder. Be sure to have at least one roleplay for each set of Barriers/Builders. (If you have more than five groups, invite other roleplays as you have time.)

❸ Encouraging Words

Objective:
To explore what Scripture has to say about how our words can discourage or encourage our teenagers (10 minutes).

Display the Scripture references you wrote out on the chalk or marker board ahead of time. Ask for volunteers to look up and read each verse aloud to the group. Discuss these Scriptures briefly, considering these questions:

- **According to these verses, in what ways can our words have a discouraging effect?** (When we use too many words—Prov. 10:19; when we our words are hyocritical or deceitful—Prov. 15:4; when we keep bringing up old problems—Prov. 17:9.)
- **In what ways can our words have an encouraging effect?** (When we use words with restraint—Prov. 17:27; when our purpose is healing—Prov. 15:4; when we urge them to live worthy lives—I Thess. 2:11, 12; when we are patient, even with our teenagers—I Thess. 5:14.)
- **Specifically, how do these verses apply to discouraging or encouraging appropriate independence and responsibility in our teens?**

When teenagers show they can handle certain responsibilities, they should be rewarded with balancing freedoms.

❹ Earning Freedom through Responsibility

Objective:

To provide a model for parents to help their teens balance freedom with responsibility; parents will also explore ways to prepare themselves personally for the letting-go process (10-25 minutes).

At this point you may be thinking, "But I need some practical help encouraging my teenagers to be more responsible. They want more freedom, all right—but they still seem so irresponsible!"

This is a common problem for parents. Most of us end up nagging—which usually goes in one ear and out the other—and then we either get angry or throw up our hands in despair. But there is a better way: helping our teens earn the freedoms they want as they fulfill greater responsibilities.

Pass out copies of "Freedoms Earned through Responsibility" (RS-9C). Explain that the chart on the top of the resource sheet is one idea for how teenagers can earn growing freedom throughout the teen years as they handle growing responsibilities appropriate to their age. Suggest that this might be done in several ways:

1. **When teenagers show they can handle certain responsibilities, they are rewarded with certain freedoms.**
2. **Or, teenagers can be given new responsibilities and new freedoms at the same time—as part of a birthday celebration, for instance. As long as responsibilities are being carried out, teenagers may enjoy their freedoms.**
3. **If the teenager fails to carry out his or her new level of responsibilities, however, the whole plan backs up to an earlier stage of responsibility and freedom. In other words, a teenager earns the level of freedom by the level of responsibility he or she carries out.**

Obviously, this chart should be adjusted to each family's situation. Instruct spouses to work together for the remainder of the session filling out the blank chart on the bottom of the resource sheet. Parents without spouses present may want to pair up for brainstorming and support as they fill out their charts. Depending upon the age of their teenagers, parents may want to fill out part of the chart with the freedoms and responsibilities their teen is already carrying out—then adding new responsibilities and freedoms to grow into.

Encourage parents to continue discussing and refining their "Freedoms Earned through Responsibility" charts at home—including their teens in the discussion (and negotiation!) if possible.

Parents should take care that the responsibilities of parenting do not overshadow their marriage relationship.

In the remaining minutes of this session, pass out "Parents Are People, Too" (RS-9D), with the following comments:

We have all heard of the "empty nest syndrome"—that is, parents who are so involved in parenting that they are not prepared for the "empty nest" when the chickens finally fly the coop. There can be a deep sense of loss—loss of the active role of parent, loss of purpose, loss of relationship. Couples may also discover that parenting has overshadowed the marriage relationship, and suddenly they are face to face with a seeming stranger.

This resource sheet lists at least three ways each of us—no matter what age our children are—can prepare ourselves for the letting-go process.

If time allows, encourage parents to prayerfully consider and write down several things they might do under each heading to help prepare themselves personally for letting go of their children in a healthy way; then encourage them to circle one new thing they could do this coming week. Otherwise, encourage parents to complete this activity at home.

Notes:

1. Adapted from Carol Kuykendall, *Learning to Let Go* (Grand Rapids, Mich.: Zondervan Publishing House, 1985), 100, 101.
2. Ibid., 99.

Building Teens' Self-Esteem

10

Session Aim:
To help parents understand the role of effective discipline and limit-setting in building their teens' self-esteem.

It is impossible to overstate the importance of healthy self-esteem in the life of a teenager. A poor self-image often leads to self-destructive behavior. It comes from feeling rejected for things we can't change, or trying to live up to unrealistic expectations, or comparing ourselves to others. Healthy self-esteem, on the other hand, is based on a realistic (rather than exaggerated) view of ourselves, the ability to accept (and be accepted for) both our strengths and our weaknesses, and being appreciated for our unique interests, gifts, and abilities.

As a child moves into adolescence, it may seem that the teenager has switched allegiances—friends are everything, the family doesn't count. But don't be fooled. Adolescents often feel very insecure in relation to their peers. They never know from day to day whether they are going to be accepted or rejected. The friends who are laughing with you one day may be laughing at you the next.

Parents can do a lot to develop a positive self-image in their teenager. Our teens need the security of knowing they are loved, accepted unconditionally, and will always belong.

—*Charles Bradshaw*

esearch has shown that a sense of personal significance is a basic human need.

Getting Ready

Scriptures:
Colossians 3:21; Luke 16:10-12; Ephesians 6:4

1. Have a supply of blank paper on hand.
2. Prepare three "signs" with both words and Scripture references which read: (1) BUILD SELF-ESTEEM—Colossians 3:21; (2) BUILD RESPONSIBILITY—Luke 16:10-12; (3) BUILD FAMILY AS SUPPORT GROUP—Ephesians 6:4.
3. Prepare copies of "Setting Limits" (RS-10A) and "Blueprint for Building Self-Esteem" (RS-10B). Make additional copies of the "Blueprint for Building Self-Esteem" so that parents with more than one teen can have one per teenager.

❶ I Am Somebody! (I Hope)

Objective:
To help parents understand the importance of a healthy self-image and the three dimensions of self-esteem (10 minutes).

Hand out sheets of blank paper to all group members and instruct them to write at the top, "My Teen Is . . ." Then tell them they have two minutes to write down as many words and phrases as they can that describe their teen. (If the group members have more than one teen, they should choose one; or spouses might each describe a different teen.)

At the end of two minutes, tell the group to put a plus (+) or minus (-) sign by each word or phrase, depending on whether it is a positive or a negative characteristic. (Some characteristics may be both!) Give the group another minute to evaluate their lists in this way.

When you sense they are done, share the following:

Both social and medical research have shown that a sense of personal significance is a basic human need. "Pioneering psychologist Alfred Adler found that when human beings feel no sense of belonging or importance, they behave in ways that provide them with a false sense of significance."[1] This can be seen in behavior as simple as "acting out" in order to get attention, to engaging in self-destructive behavior—alcohol or drug abuse, sexual activity, or joining gangs—to create some sense of identity and belonging.

Ask the group members to look at the list of characteristics they did a moment ago. Is it heavy on negative characteristics? If so, parents may be reflecting back to their teen a negative self-image. For example: **If your child tends to be clumsy, as adolescents often are, you may say in exasperation, "How come you're always so clumsy!" Your teen begins to believe, "I'm a clumsy person." The prophecy becomes self-fulfilling.**

Now ask the group members to consider the positive characteristics on their list. **If your teen is generous, hard working, humorous, tender, or honest—does your teen know you appreciate these qualities in him or her? It's easy to let our teens know when they've blown it, but we often forget to let them know what we appreciate.**

On the chalk or marker board draw three overlapping circles as shown here. Write the words within each circle as you briefly define self-esteem:

Just what is self-esteem? Self-esteem is how we feel about who we are, and how we see ourselves in relation to other people. We may have low self-esteem based on a negative self-image, or we may have high self-esteem based on a positive self-image. Our self-image generally develops in three areas.

Define the three dimensions of self-esteem as follows:

• *A sense of belonging* means **"having a sense of security and identity with others who love, accept, and support me."[2] A sense of belonging begins early in a child's life, developing a family identity which gives roots and a feeling of security. These feelings include feeling safe, cared for, accepted, and supported. If the sense of belonging is weak in the family, a teenager will look for it elsewhere.**

• *A sense of worth* means **"being affirmed as a person of value; being cherished and respected."[3] A teenager's identity has two parts: being accepted as part of a group (belonging) and being valued as someone unique and different. This second aspect of self-esteem has the most to do with who we are. We have a sense of importance and worth based simply on who we are, not on our performance. If a teenager does not feel valued, he or she may engage in destructive behavior because "no one cares."**

f teens continually experience failure in spite of their efforts to do right or to accomplish something, their self-esteem withers.

• *A sense of competence* means "gaining a sense of achievement; being affirmed as a capable person."[4] If teens continually experience failure in spite of their efforts to do things right or to accomplish something, their self-esteem withers. Everyone—not just teens— needs that feeling of satisfaction and fulfillment: "I can do it!" "I did it!" A teenager who doesn't feel capable may give up and quit trying to please.

❷ Effective Discipline and Self-Esteem

Objective:
To brainstorm a variety of discipline methods and evaluate their effectiveness in building healthy self-esteem (20 minutes).

At this point, pause and point out the following:

In Sessions 8 and 9, the primary focus was on preparing teens to leave home as responsible young adults. Along the way, of course, teens are testing the limits (and their parents!), which always brings up the question, "What about discipline?" Discipline might seem a separate subject from developing responsibility and healthy self-esteem, but in fact they are very much related.

For starters, ask the group to brainstorm different types of discipline—both positive and negative—used with teenagers (all ages). Questions to help start the process:

• **What kinds of discipline did you experience as teenagers?**

• **What kinds of discipline have you used with your own teens?**

• **What do other parents do?**

Encourage the group to list all types of discipline, whether they agree with it or not, or have used it or not. (Ask a volunteer to record these ideas on the chalk or marker board.)

You might want to suggest some of the following if they don't get mentioned:

• Cutting allowance
• Yelling
• Threatening
• Negotiating (contract)
• Grounding
• Restricting other activities
• Giving positive rewards
• Assigning additional chores
• Losing privileges
• Holding a family meeting
• Spanking/hitting
• Humiliating put-downs
• Giving the silent treatment
• Assigning community service
• Going on a parental strike
• Lecturing
• Forcing an apology
• Bribing

T
he discipline method we use should build self-esteem, responsibility, and the family as a support group."

After two or three minutes of brainstorming, ask three volunteers who have Bibles to come to the front and sit facing the rest of the group. Give each of these volunteers one of the "signs" you prepared ahead of time and ask them to look up the Scripture printed on it. Then say to the group:

In his book, *Teen Shaping,* **youth pastor Len Kageler says that the disciplinary methods we use should accomplish three things in the lives of our young people: (1) Build self-esteem; (2) Build responsibility; and (3) Build the family as a support group.**[5]

Ask volunteers to hold up their signs and read their assigned Scripture verse.

Let's evaluate our list of discipline methods for how well they accomplish these important factors.

Circle one of the disciplinary methods recorded on the chalkboard—such as "lecturing." The group members should decide whether any, all, or none of the three "builders" are accomplished by that method—and why they think so. When one or more of the "builders" is suggested, the person with that sign should hold it up so the whole group can have a visual image of what is accomplished by that discipline method. (If other group members disagree, you might suggest the person put the sign back down; or, the sign could be held "low," "high," or "halfway," depending upon whether the group thinks the discipline method accomplishes that factor "a lot," "a little," or "sometimes.")

Continue this evaluation with as many of the discipline methods as possible in the time available. Some examples suggested by Kageler:[6]

- *Losing privileges:* if logically related to misbehavior, it can build responsibility.
- *Cutting allowance:* (none).
- *Grounding:* if logically related to misbehavior, it can build responsibility. Otherwise, (none).
- *Negotiating (contract):* If teen honors or fulfills contract, it can build self-esteem; build responsibility; and build the family as a support group.
- *Bribing:* (none).
- *Giving positive rewards:* affirmation for positive behavior or choices can build self-esteem; build responsibility; and build the family as a support group.
- *Yelling/Threatening:* (none).

A

s children become teenagers, parental discipline should move into parental discipleship.

❸ Limit Setting

Objective:
To help parents think through guidelines for setting limits for teenagers (5-15 minutes).

After the discussion on effective (and not-so effective) discipline methods, parents may appreciate some additional help in knowing how to set limits for their teens. Pass out "Setting Limits" (RS-10A) with the following comments:

Even though teenagers are nearing physical and intellectual maturity, they still need a good deal of parental guidance. This includes setting some specific limits. Many parents tend toward one of two extremes. Some establish rigid rules in order to maintain control during the trying teen years, while others conclude that since teenagers are approaching adulthood, they should make their own decisions.

The biblical standard is somewhere between the extremes. As children become teenagers, parental discipline should move into parental discipleship. Teenagers are too big to spank, but they are old enough to respond to logic, persuasion, fairness, interest, positive reinforcement, love, parental example, and the power of prayer.

If time allows, ask volunteers to read the eight guidelines aloud to the group. After each guideline, encourage the group members to share any questions, observations, or personal experience regarding that guideline, generating a group discussion. Otherwise, encourage couples to read and discuss these guidelines together at home; single parents could discuss them with another parent or supportive friend.

❹ Building Self-Esteem

Objective:
Parents will plan specific ways to build self-esteem in their teenagers (10-15 minutes).

Up to this point we have talked in generalities concerning the importance of self-esteem. Now let's brainstorm specific things we as parents can do to build self-esteem in our teens.

Divide the group members into three small groups (size doesn't matter), appointing a recorder for each group. Ask one group to come up with as many ideas as they can in five minutes to build up a teen's sense of belonging. The second group should brainstorm ideas to build up a teen's sense of worth; the third, a teen's sense of competence. Encourage the groups to be very specific. Also remind the groups that the rule of brainstorming is to go for quantity of ideas, not to evaluate quality.

At the end of five minutes, call time. Then ask the recorder for each group to share its ideas. Write these briefly (using just a word or phrase) on the chalkboard in three columns labeled: *Belonging, Worth, Competence.*

Now pass out copies of "Blueprint for Building Self-Esteem" (RS-10B), so that parents have one sheet per teenager in the family. Working as couples, if possible, parents should fill in the name(s) of their teen(s) and the area of self-esteem which most needs building up.

If time allows, on the back of the resource sheet parents should list at least ten specific things to do to build up the weak area(s) in their teen's self-esteem, without neglecting the other dimension(s) of self-esteem. (The brainstorming lists still on the chalkboard should provide many ideas.)

Encourage parents to write these specific things to do in the boxes at the bottom of the page, spread out over a three-week period. Use the remainder of the time for parents to work on these sheets. What doesn't get finished should be completed at home.

Close in prayer.

Notes:

1. H. Stephen Glenn and Jane Nelsen, *Raising Self-Reliant Children in a Self-Indulgent World* (New York: St. Martin's Press, 1989), 99.
2. Norman Wakefield, *Building Self-Esteem in the Family* (Elgin, Ill.: David C. Cook Publishing Co., 1977).
3. Ibid.
4. Ibid.
5. Len Kageler, *Teen Shaping* (Old Tappan, N. J.: Fleming H. Revell Co., 1990), 56.
6. Ibid., Chapter 4.

The Night Is Young, but We Are Old

11

Session Aim:
To help parents develop an optimistic and godly view of aging.

We sometimes criticize society's obsession with youthfulness, yet nothing announces mid-life so clearly as our aging bodies. Though today's mid-lifers look healthier and "younger" than their parents did at the same age, they are finding that it is no longer easy to keep fit.

Those who don't recognize their aging process can be at risk. Backs are more easily strained. Heart attacks, while not yet common, are likely to be more dangerous when they do occur, especially among men who may still behave as though they have no physical limits. Cancer among both women and men becomes a real possibility, but if caught early, there is a good chance for cure. Those in mid-life accumulate excess weight more easily, shed it with greater effort, and face accompanying medical complications.

Except for golfers, most professional athletes have faced a mid-career transition by this age. Other people in careers which rely on their physical abilities or appearances must adjust, if not change jobs, by this time.

Facing an aging body can produce depression and anxiety, or it can be a time of acceptance and adjustment. There are also assets that improve with age—a cause for celebration!

*T*hose who don't recognize their aging process can be at risk.

Getting Ready

Scriptures:
Job 12:12; Psalm 23:6;
92:12-14; 148:7, 12;
Proverbs 16:31; Isaiah 46:4;
John 10:10b

1. Make enough photocopies of "Are You over the Hill?" (RS-11A) and "Coming to Terms with Mid-Life" (RS-11B).
2. Have extra paper and pencils available.
3. Down the left side of your chalk or marker board list the following verses:
   Job 12:12
   Psalm 23:6
   Psalm 92:12-14
   Psalm 148:7, 12
   Proverbs 16:31
   Isaiah 46:4
   John 10:10b

❶ Our Bodies— Friend or Foe?

Objective:
To help the group members face their body's aging process (5 minutes).

Ask the group members if they have heard the story Charles Swindoll tells about the guy who fell in love with an opera singer: **"He hardly knew her, since his only view of the singer was through binoculars—from the third balcony. But he was convinced he could live 'happily ever after' married to a voice like that. He scarcely noticed she was considerably older than he. Nor did he care that she walked with a limp. Her mezzo-soprano voice would take them through whatever might come. After a whirlwind romance and a hurry-up ceremony, they were off for their honeymoon together.**

"She began to prepare for their first night together. As he watched, his chin dropped to his chest. She plucked out her glass eye and plopped it into a container on the nightstand. She pulled off her wig, ripped off her false eyelashes, yanked out her dentures, unstrapped her artificial leg, and smiled at him as she slipped off her glasses that hid her hearing aid. Stunned and horrified, he gasped, 'For goodness sake, woman, *sing, sing, SING!'* "[1]

Ask the group members how many feel like the opera singer where age is starting to rob them of some of their physical assets. Assure those who agree that they are not alone. Distribute copies of "Are You over the Hill?" (RS-11A) and draw attention to the statistics at the top of the page showing how some people have tried to "fight" their body's aging.

Between growth and aging, aging takes up about three-quarters of our life.

Explain that between growth and aging, aging takes up about three-quarters of our life. The fastest growth takes place in the life of the unborn child. Growing is also rapid in the infant and the young child, with another growth spurt at puperty, but is progressively slower until about age twenty-one, when it peaks. Growth now begins to change toward decline. We are not very aware of any decline in our twenties and early thirties. Though we slow down a bit, we may jokingly pass it off.

But as we hit forty, we begin to identify our bodies as an enemy that makes us look and feel old.

❷ Over The Hill?

Objective:
To help the group members get a realistic picture of what it means to be middle-aged (15 minutes).

Ask the group members to mark the statements true or false at the bottom of "Are You over the Hill?" (RS-11A). When most seem to be done, read through the statements, asking for a show of hands indicating agreement or disagreement with each statement. Invite those who make the correct choice to offer reasons. You may also want to add the relevant information that follows.[2]

1. The overall health of a person in his or her forties sharply declines. (False)

- The overall health of a person does not sharply decline, but the types of problems may change. For example, the frequency of illness and disability go up with the years, but the frequency of accidents goes down.
- Generally, older adults tire faster, have higher blood pressure and more dental problems, and need more time to recuperate from fatigue or illness. However, they are less susceptible to colds and allergies.
- Except for the remarkable long lives of some ancient biblical characters, human life expectancy has increased through the ages. For example, people are thought to have lived an average of only eighteen years in the Bronze Age and only twenty years in ancient Greece. Life expectancy had grown to thirty-one in the Middle Ages, and to thirty-seven by the eighteenth century. In 1900, average life expectancy in the United States was forty-seven, and only 3 percent of the population lived past sixty-five. Today, life expectancy is seventy-five.[3]

2. The years of greatest productivity in various professions are between twenty-eight and thirty-two. (False)

- Harvey C. Lehman, professor of psychology at Ohio University, made the most comprehensive survey of this question. He studied the years of greatest productivity in various professions, arts, and sciences. His research,[4] which took twenty years to complete, suggests that the age of greatest proficiency in science, mathematics, and practical invention is thirty-three to forty-four. The most productive years for physicians and medical researchers were between thirty-five and thirty-nine. The peak years for psychologists were from thirty-five to thirty-nine.
- Most painters and composers, however, do their best work before the age of thirty-five.
- Though some of your most creative years are likely to be in your thirties, you are likely to earn more money during your middle fifties than at any other period in your life. Other wide-scale studies on the earning power of various age groups, conducted at Ohio University, have shown that, under current conditions, one's earned income is likely to be greatest at about fifty-five or fifty-six. A further survey made at the same university showed that the ages of most of the nation's top-flight executives range between fifty-five and sixty.

3. A person can learn anything more quickly during the early twenties than at any other time of your life. (True)

- Studies conducted at Columbia University show that a person's ability to learn increases from early childhood up to the age of twenty-five. After that time, it was found that the ability to absorb knowledge diminishes about one percent per year.
- Our ability to learn begins to diminish, but our ability to think and reason continues to increase with age, provided we exercise these faculties sufficiently.
- Studies conducted at several universities show that the average person's mental abilities decrease with age, but this is largely due to most people letting their brains get "rusty" after they get out of school.
- At the University of Minnesota, investigators studied 5,500 extension-course students, whose ages ranged from twenty to seventy and were in occupations that made continual demands on their intelligence. In the vast majority of cases,

mental ability definitely increased with age. The average person of forty had appreciably more "on the ball" than the person of thirty; the person in his fifties scored higher than the one of forty-five, and so on.

- Reportedly, as few as ten percent of our brain cells disappear, even over a long lifetime. It is only the fear that you are too old to learn new tricks that limits you, not any lack of cerebral capacity.

4. A person's greatest physical strength is experienced in one's twenties. (True)

- A consensus of university studies shows that physical strength increases steadily with each passing year until you reach your middle twenties. But after the age of twenty-five, your muscular powers diminish—so gradually at first that you are scarcely aware of being less strong than you were. As age increases, your strength declines at an increasingly rapid rate. Most of this weakening occurs in the back and leg muscles, less in the arm muscles.

5. The average person's physical appearance changes in mid-life. (True)

- The most obvious signs of mid-life are, for most people, readily apparent in the mirror. Except for style, there may be little change in the way people look during early adulthood, but middle age is usually characterized by substantial alterations in appearance.

go to your
H. S. reunions ←

- There is an increased tendency toward weight gain and a redistribution of fat in the body. While body fat is only 10 percent of body weight in most adolescents, it is often 20 percent by middle age, and most of it settles around the waist. The bust or chest becomes smaller, and the abdomen and hips larger.

- Usually during the forties, the hairline recedes—particularly in men—and the hair thins out. Baldness increases, again, mostly in men. Graying hair increases about the same time, so that by the fifties most men and women are gray-haired, and some are even white-haired.

God is not exclusively youth-oriented. He loves and cares for people at every stage of life.

❸ God's View of Aging

Objective:
To help parents realize that aging is an important and productive stage of life in God's plan (15 minutes).

Redirect the group's attention from what researchers and doctors say about aging to God's view. Ask the parents to work in pairs as they study the Bible verses listed on the board. Suggest that half the group start with the first verse and work down while the other half start at the bottom and work up—to be sure all verses are covered in your allotted time. Provide pencils and paper for any who need them.

After eight minutes ask for their findings, writing them on the board beside the references. Their discoveries may look something like this:

Job 12:12—*(With age comes wisdom and understanding.)*
Psalm 23:6—*(God's loving goodness is with us always.)*
Psalm 92:12-14—*(We can be productive in old age.)*
Psalm 148:7, 12—*(God includes old age in His plan.)*
Proverbs 16:31—*(To be a godly older person is an honor.)*
Isaiah 46:4—*(God cares for us in old age.)*
John 10:10b—*(God did not put an age limit on His promise of abundant life.)*

Summarize the Bible study with the following comments:
God is not exclusively youth-oriented. He loves and cares for people at every stage of life. He ministers to us so that our lives can continue to be productive, as well as contented. We have also seen that His promises are not conditional on being young. They are for all people at all ages.

❹ It's Not Really So Bad

Objective:
To help mid-life parents evaluate how satisfied they are in various areas of life and to design goals for changing or accepting unsatisfactory elements (10-25 minutes).

The sooner we come to terms with the realities of mid-life—including life not turning out as we had hoped—the easier the transition will be. As we have seen, God considers a bigger picture in looking at a person's life, and from that perspective, age can have some decided benefits. We need to gain that broader view.

Distribute copies of "Coming to Terms with Mid-Life" (RS-11B) and explain that one way to face the adjustments that come with mid-life is to evaluate what changes have taken place in the last few years and whether their impact on various areas of life is more or less satisfying.

Allow the remaining time for group members to work individually on the questionnaire. If time allows, instruct the group members to use the goal setting skills they learned in Session 2 to establish plans for changing or accepting unsatisfactory elements identified on "Coming to Terms with Mid-Life" (RS-11B). Tell them to begin with the two most unsatisfactory conditions and work on others as time allows.

Encourage group members to review the long- and short-term goals they formulated in Session 2, using "My Mission Statement" (RS-2C) and "Stepping-Stones" (RS-2D), if they have them available.

Close the session by leading the group in praying this version of the Serenity Prayer: **"Lord, give me the courage to accept the things I cannot change, the strength to change the things I can, and the wisdom to know the difference."**

Notes:

1. As quoted by Marion Duckworth in *Strike the Original Match: a Life Topics Study* (Elgin, Ill.: David C. Cook Publishing Co., 1992), 40.

2. Adapted from Charles Bradshaw, *You and Your Teen* (Elgin, Ill.: David C. Cook Publishing Co., 1985), 48, 49.

3. "The New Middle Age," *Newsweek*, Dec. 7, 1992, 52.

4. As reported by Judith Stevens-Long in *Adult Life: Developmental Process* (Palo Alto, Calif.: Mayfield Publishing Co., 1979), 359-360.

Honoring Your Aging Parents

12

Session Aim:
To help group members explore three major issues of aging parents and determine which issue needs attention with their own parents.

Mid-life people feel increasingly responsible for aging parents. The parents have always been the strong generation, but now all that changes.

The first change is role reversal. Parents gradually become the dependents and adult children become the caretakers. Not only is it hard to think of parents unable to manage for themselves, but mid-lifers feel torn. Though they want to provide for the comfort and happiness of their parents, they'd like to keep disruption of their life to a minimum.

Where parents live is the second issue. Some parents feel more secure in their own home with familiar surroundings. For others, a retirement village is ideal. Sometimes, a special-care facility is necessary. And there's always the question of whether Mom or Dad should move in with an adult child. Shortages of space or money (or both) complicate solutions.

The third issue is the approaching death of one's parents. Psychologist Abraham Maslow said, "One learns more from the death of a parent than from all the academic studies." When parents are living, we feel protected from our own death because one always thinks the parents will die first. But when they die, we feel next in line.

—*Charles Bradshaw*

Some interactions with your parents will be positive; others will involve conflict and negative feelings.

Getting Ready

Scriptures:
Ephesians 6:2, 3; I Timothy 5:8

1. Make photocopies of "My Parents' Situation" (RS-12A), "Role Reversal" (RS-12B), "Where Will They Live?" (RS-12C), and "When One Parent Dies" (RS-12D).
2. Cut the last three resource sheets in half, but keep the top and bottom of each sheet with each other so you can hand out both halves at one time.

❶ My Parents Are Aging

Objective:
To encourage group members to get a realistic picture of their own parents' current status in life (10-25 minutes).

Each describe their Parent situations ✗

Introduce this session with the following comments:
Growing older involves having to make changes. Not only do you change, but your parents are changing, too. And some of their changes may trouble you.

If your parents live nearby, you may be aware of the ways they are changing; if they live far away, the changes they are experiencing may surprise you at each visit. Let's take a few minutes and evaluate our own parents' status in life in several areas.

Pass out copies of "My Parents' Situation" (RS-12A), asking the group members to write a sentence or two after each category describing their parents' current status in that area. Tell them to begin with their biological parents, if they are living, and substitute in-laws or other older relatives for whom they feel responsible where there are gaps.

Allow five minutes for the group members to work individually. When most seem done, have them put a check (✓) beside each category that represents a recent or impending change for their parents.

Explain that how mid-life parents handle changes concerning their aging parents may be influenced by their own past relationships or their observation of their parents' relationship to grandparents at a similar age.

Memories will affect your present actions and feelings. If you have loving, giving parents, you respect them and can accept their weaknesses. If you have a negative relationship with your parents, you may feel anger and resentment at having to help someone who has done little for you.

No matter how you feel, you will experience mixed emotions. Some interactions with your parents will be positive; others will involve conflict and negative feelings. However, the more we understand the aging pro-

cess and know what issues are likely to arise, the better we will be able to resolve some of these issues and cope with the changing relationship between ourselves and our aging parents.

Also point out that their teenagers are observing the relationship between their parents and grandparents. In many ways, mid-life parents are modeling how they will likely be treated by their own adult children some day.

Invite testimonies from the group members of either ideal or undesirable ways these conditions were met in the previous generation (parents to grandparents).

If time allows, instruct the group members to choose partners (spouses where possible) and tell them each to select one of the issues identified by a check mark on the resource sheet representing a recent or impending change for their parents and brainstorm with their spouse or partner a few specific actions or attitudes to help them resolve that issue.

❷ Issues with Aging Parents

Objective:
To explore three issues of aging parents, determine how each affects the parents now, and discuss possible solutions (30 minutes).

Use as case studies?

①

Divide the group into teams of three people each. Instruct the teams that they will be doing three roleplays in which they trade roles. In each roleplay, one team member is to be the aging parent and the other two are to be mid-life relatives—for example, a married son and daughter-in-law, or an adult daughter and son, etc. That configuration will change so that each participant has a chance to play the role of the aging parent, but instruct the teams to choose who will be the first to play the aging parent before you pass out the roleplays. After the first roleplay, that role will rotate clockwise.

Distribute the first roleplay, "Role Reversal" (RS-12B), giving the top half to the designated "senior citizen" and the bottom half to be shared by the "adult children." Allow the teams to play out the situation in their small group for three minutes, then interrupt and ask the following questions for group response.

1. How did this situation make you feel? Irritated? Sad? Overwhelmed? Amused? Angry? Upset? Solicit responses from both the aging parents and the adult children.

2. What can you learn from this situation in terms of how best to manage role reversals with aging parents? Answers might include:

If you have your parents move in with you, settle beforehand that the head of the household sets the rules—not the oldest person.

- Don't get hooked by the controlling nature of their needs.
- Aging parents need emotional support in the midst of their increasing dependency.
- They need help adjusting socially.
- They should be encouraged to adjust, rather than give up.

Now distribute the second roleplay, "Where Will They Live?" (RS-12C), giving the top half to the second designated "senior citizen" and the bottom to be shared by the "adult children." Allow the teams to play out the situation among themselves for three minutes, then ask the following questions.

1. Aside from cost, what should you consider in having aging parents move into a retirement center? Answers might include:

- Parents' wishes.
- Whether the reduced responsibilities would accelerate their decline.
- Whether removing them from familiar settings and close friends would be too traumatic.
- The quality of care and services available.

2. If you were to have parents move in with you, what would be the primary considerations? In his video series, *Crises of Transition*, Dr. DeLoss Friesen suggests:

- Do not have a parent move in if it is going to harm your marriage.
- Differences must be resolved before, not after, the move.
- Do not have parents move in if they can care for themselves independently.
- Specify responsibilities and expectations beforehand.
- Settle beforehand that the head of the household sets the rules—not the oldest person.

Distribute the third roleplay, "When One Parent Dies" (RS-12D), giving the top half to the third designated "senior citizen" and the bottom to be shared by the "adult children." Allow the teams to play out the situation for three minutes, then ask the following questions.

1. How does the death of this spouse/parent affect your feelings about the possibility of your own death? Guide the discussion until group members are talking about the awareness that they may be next in line.

During mid-life, a person must not only accept the reality of death but also the fact that one's mate may die first.

2. What are some ways people respond to their impending death? In his book, *Men in Mid-Life Crisis,* Jim Conway suggests the following common responses.

- A person may deny that he or she is going to die because death is linked with old age, and he or she is still trying to deny the aging process.
- A person may accept defeat. People may be so discouraged by the reality of eventual death that they may give up the desire to continue living.
- People may find themselves overcome with the fear of death, because they are unprepared to face life after death or because of a lack of information about what happens in death. "Does it hurt to die? Will I still want to live even when I'm dying?" Every person must work through each of these anxieties, getting factual information to prepare for the stage of acceptance.
- Acceptance of death. Coming fully to accept one's ultimate death gives a serene quality to life and prepares a person to enjoy life more completely.[1]

During mid-life, a person must not only accept the reality of death but also the fact that one's mate may die first. If one can accept this, there is a valuing of hours and days that gives a special, loving intensity that might not be realized if the death of one's mate is feared or denied.

NOTE: You might want to recommend the following books for additional reading: *Facing Death and the Life After* by Billy Graham (Word, Inc., 1982) and *Through the Wilderness of Loneliness* by Tim Hansel (David C. Cook Publishing Co., 1991).

❸ The Needs of Aging Parents

Objective:
To help mid-life parents identify the major issues they face with their aging parents and select one specific action/attitude to improve (10 minutes).

Ask the group to look up Ephesians 6:2, 3 and select a volunteer to read the verses aloud.

Do these verses apply to the way you relate to your aging parents or only to the way your children relate to you? (These verses relate to all parent-child relationships; our responsibility to honor our parents never stops.)

Next, ask the group to look up I Timothy 5:8, choosing a volunteer to read the verse aloud.

Communicate in your aging parents' "language of love," in the way that makes them feel good.

What do honoring and providing for your aging parents involve?

Start the discussion by emphasizing that provision means more than financial support. As the discussion proceeds, ask what "honor" and "provision" mean in the following areas:

1. **Respect.** (Consulting them for advice, recounting their accomplishments, listening to the old stories, giving them some special care.)
2. **Contact.** (Freedom from abandonment—a common fear of the elderly. Do not forget physical touch.)
3. **Security.** (Security from outside danger, assurance that you'll be there if they run out of money, etc.)
4. **Worry.** (Accept their tendency to worry while balancing it with your optimism. Reassure them as they have reassured you in the past.)
5. **Love.** (Communicate in their language of love. What makes *them* feel loved?)
6. **The need to be needed.** (From childhood to death, the consciousness that we are wanted and needed—not just tolerated—is the most powerful support for self-respect and the will to live.)

Close the session in prayer. If time allows, encourage group members to choose a partner (spouses, if possible) to pray for each other about relating to their aging parents in a positive and godly way.

Notes:

1. Jim Conway, *Men in Mid-Life Crisis* (Elgin, Ill.: David C. Cook Publishing Co., 1978), 268, 269.

Hanging In There

13

Session Aim:
To challenge each person to make decisions that will assist him or her in the healthy resolution of mid-life issues.

Gilbert Brim, team leader for the Research Network on Successful Midlife Development debunks the notion of a mid-life "crisis." "It's such a mushy concept," he chides, "not like a clinical diagnosis in the medical field." But he concedes it conveniently allows people to blame something external for their feelings and behavior.[1]

It's reassuring that mid-life needn't be a crisis, but it can still be rough. Jim Conway, in his book, *Men in Mid-Life Crisis*, said: "If a man interacts with the mid-life crisis fully, it can be the most profitable experience to prepare him for his own retirement. As he comes to a peaceful self-image, an enthusiastic relationship with his mate, as he adjusts his career to fit his life and works through pressures with his children and parents, he will find that his emotional work is the best preparation for what society calls retirement. If, on the other hand, a man does not face these concerns in mid-life, they will grow, and when he is pushed out of a job, it will be as if the world collapses around him."[2]

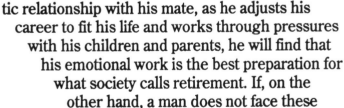

In mid-life, failure *of* plans is not the tragedy; the failure *to* plan is. Remember Winston Churchill's speech: "Never Give Up. Never Give Up. Never Give Up. Never Give Up."

—*Charles Bradshaw*

*I*n mid-life, failure of *plans is not the tragedy; the failure* to *plan is.*

Getting Ready

Scripture:
Psalm 121

1. Obtain as many envelopes as you have group members. Make a copy of the "Biography Game" (RS-13A) for each participant. Cut the "cards" apart and put eight *identical* cards in each envelope. If the number of people in your group is not divisible by eight, you will have some cards left over. Divide these cards equally for the remaining envelopes, putting as many identical cards as possible in each envelope (for instance, six of one card and two of another).
2. Make copies of "A Baker's Dozen of Helpful Hints" (RS-13B) and "Smoothing the Mid-Life Transition" (RS-13C).
3. Write the themes of the four units of this course on the chalk or marker board:
   Unit 1: Growing with the Challenges of Mid-Life
   Unit 2: Growing a Family Team
   Unit 3: Launching Your Young Adult
   Unit 4: Growing Older with Dignity

❶ Try, Try Again

Objective:
To illustrate the importance of moving ahead without fear of failure (15-20 minutes).

Give each group member an envelope with instructions not to open it until you say start. Then tell the group that they are going to play the Biography Game. Have them stand up and push back the chairs—whatever is necessary to provide room to circulate.

Explain the game as follows:

In each envelope there are eight cards with biography statements on them. The object is to trade your cards with other people until you have a full set of eight different cards. The trading is accomplished by yelling how many cards you want to trade, such as: "One! One! One!" or "Three! Three! Three!" until you find another person with a similar number to trade. (NOTE: if making noise is a problem in your setting, group members can whisper or hold up the number of fingers to indicate the number of cards to be traded.) **Of course, if you have three to trade but can only find someone offering two, you can adjust your number down. But never give away more cards than you get, or you will end up with less than eight.**

The cards you offer must be alike, but do not reveal which cards they are. From the cards you receive, retain only what you need, and trade the rest until you have a full set of eight different cards.

When your set is complete, arrange them in order, and guess the historical person they describe. Then yell STORY!

At that moment, the trading *must stop*. The winner will read the story and tell who it describes.

If you are wrong, the trading starts again until someone else gets a full set, reads the story again, and correctly identifies the subject.

(NOTE to leader: The correct answer is Abraham Lincoln, whose only term as President of the United States was cut short by his assassination.)

When the group understands the game, give the start signal, and be ready to judge who wins.

After the game, have the group be seated and draw attention to how many times Lincoln seemed to fail. Note that he is an excellent example that failure is not the worst thing that can happen to us.

For instance, in scientific research multiple "failures" commonly lead to success. The combined unsuccessful experiments of Marie Curie, Alexander Fleming, and Louis Pasteur run into the thousands. It would have been easy for any one of them to give up after the first hundred failures or so, but today we might have no radium, no penicillin, and no pasteurized milk.

Tell the group members to choose a partner sitting nearby. Encourage each person to share with his or her partner at least one "fear of failure" related to the area of mid-life changes. Each partner should take no more than two minutes.

❷ Helpful Hints

Objective:
To help parents apply helpful hints for a profitable mid-life to their own situations
(15 minutes).

Distribute copies of "A Baker's Dozen of Helpful Hints" (RS-13B). Explain that the resource sheet contains suggestions by Dr. Gary Collins from his book, *Spotlight on Stress*. Invite the group members to help each other by applying them to mid-life.

Introduce each suggestion with a question as listed here. You can summarize the group's responses with the comments following the questions.

1. Why is it important not to play roles? (Trying hard to be the "liberated woman" or the "smooth businessman," for example, will only create stress because you are not being yourself.)

When you move more slowly, you feel less pressured. So, slow down!

2. How might choosing our friends wisely smooth our mid-life transitions? (People who are critical or constant complainers can tear down your spirit, whereas people with a positive outlook on life can be an encouraging oasis during times of stress.)

3. Why shouldn't we let things drift? (Procrastination and indecision only guarantee misery. If there is unhappiness or worry in your life, it's better to face it and try to do something about the problem.)

4. What happens when we admit our fears? (Facing our fears lessens their impact; admitting them to a spouse or supportive friends can help bring perspective.)

5. Why should we make time to get away? (If we are too busy or in a rut, mid-life transitions can sweep us along without adequate prayer, reflection, planning, or decision-making. A few minutes of privacy each day, a half-day retreat, or a getaway weekend when you can relax and think, can keep us in touch with where we want to go, and why.)

6. Why should we be willing to compromise? (Compromise is a sign of strength, not weakness. To be rigid, to refuse to give in, or to insist on winning, all create tension.)

7. What are the benefits of seeking a balance in our life? (Work, leisure, physical exercise, contemplation, and resting are all part of life. You can overdo any of these, just as you can avoid some of them. Both alternatives create stress.)

8. Why must we be realistic? (Unrealized expectations create constant dissatisfaction. Recognize that you can change some things but not others.)

9. Why take one thing at a time? (Trying to do everything at once means we either get overloaded, or we feel so overwhelmed we do nothing. Start with the most important or difficult task and go from there. If helpful, make lists and cross things off as they are accomplished.)

10. How can we slow down? (Practice moving more slowly. Slow your speech when you talk and your pace when you walk. Eat with slower movements, putting down your fork between bites. Drive below the speed limit and stop for yellow lights. When you move more slowly, you feel less pressured.)

11. Why should we avoid excuses? (Blaming others or circumstances only keeps us irritated and doesn't help much. Taking responsibility for yourself and your own actions gives you more control over your life.)

*I*f you build on your strong points and work at improving the weak areas, you will feel more accepting of yourself.

12. What's the benefit of talking things over? (A spouse, friend, relative, pastor, or professional counselor can often help you see things that are unclear otherwise. Don't be afraid to turn to these sources for help.)

13. What is the benefit of a realistic self-image? (It's hard work trying to live up to unrealistic expectations for yourself. All of us have both strong and weak points. If you build on your strong points and work at improving the weak areas, you will feel more accepting of yourself while growing in self-confidence.)

❸ Bringing It On Home

Objective:
To help parents evaluate the mid-life challenges they are experiencing in light of the tasks of making a successful transition (15-25 minutes).

Encourage the group members to reflect on the major areas covered in previous sessions by noting the unit themes you have written on the chalk or marker board.

Pass out copies of "Smoothing the Mid-Life Transition" (RS-13C) and ask the group to divide into pairs with someone other than a spouse. Tell partners to take turns interviewing each other concerning the main topics that have been covered during this course, using the questions labeled, "Interview 1." Answers should be as brief as possible; the interviewer should briefly record his or her partner's answers on the resource sheet. Warn the teams that there will be only five minutes for each interview.

After five minutes, call time and have interviewer and interviewee change roles.

If time allows, instruct partners to now interview each other regarding the elements required to make a successful transition, using the questions labeled "Interview 2," again allowing five minutes for each interview.

When you have five minutes remaining in the session, prayerfully read Psalm 121 as an encouragement and blessing. Then encourage partners to close the session with specific prayer for each other, using the last question of "Interview 1" as a guide.

Notes:

1. Melinda Beck, "The New Middle Age," *Newsweek*, December 7, 1992, 52.
2. Jim Conway, *Men in Mid-Life Crisis* (Elgin, Ill.: David C. Cook Publishing Co., 1978), 263.

Bibliography

Augsburger, David. *Sustaining Love: Healing & Growth in the Passages of Marriage.* Ventura, Calif.: Regal Books, 1988.

Conway, Jim. *Men in Mid-Life Crisis.* Elgin, Ill.: David C. Cook Publishing Co., 1978.

Conway, Jim and Sally. *Women in Mid-Life Crisis.* Wheaton, Ill.: Tyndale House Publishers, Inc., 1983.

Glenn, H. Stephen and Nelsen, Jane. *Raising Self-Reliant Children in a Self-Indulgent World.* Rocklin, Calif.: Prima Publishing & Communications, 1989. Also available from New York, N.Y.: St. Martin's Press.

Graham, Billy, *Facing Death and the Life After.* Irving, Texas: Word, Inc., 1982.

Hansel, Tim, *Through the Wilderness of Loneliness.* Elgin, Ill.: David C. Cook Publishing Co., 1991.

Howard, J. Grant. *Balancing Life's Demands.* Portland, Ore.: Multnomah Press, 1983.

Jenkins, Jerry. *Loving Your Marriage Enough to Protect It.* Chicago: Moody Press, 1993.

Kageler, Len. *Teen Shaping.* Old Tappan, N. J.: Fleming H. Revell Co., 1990.

Kuykendall, Carol. *Learning to Let Go.* Grand Rapids, Mich.: Zondervan Publishing House, 1985.

Laurent, Dr. Robert. *Bringing Your Teen Back to God.* Elgin, Ill.: David C. Cook Publising Co., 1991.

_____. *Keeping Your Teen in Touch with God.* Elgin, Ill.: David C. Cook Publising Co., 1991.

Lush, Jean, with Vredevelt, Pam. *Women and Stress: A Practical Approach to Managing Tension.* Grand Rapids, Mich.: Revell, 1992.

Smalley, Gary. *For Better or For Best.* Grand Rapids, Mich.: Zondervan Publishing House, 1988.

Swindoll, Charles R. *Strike the Original Match.* Portland, Ore.: Multnomah Press, 1980.

Wright, H. Norman. *Seasons of a Marriage.* Ventura, Calif.: Regal Books, 1982.

Mid-Life Is . . .

Note: Make one photocopy of this resource sheet, then cut apart the seven quotes on the dotted lines. Save this master copy intact.

- Cut Here - ✂

Mid-life is . . .   the time when a man is always thinking that in a week or two he will feel as good as ever. *—Don Marquis*

- Cut Here -

Mid-life is . . .   when you are too young to get on Social Security and too old to get another job.

- Cut Here -

Mid-life is . . .   when you're sitting at home on a Saturday night and the telephone rings and you hope it isn't for you. *—Ogden Nash*

- Cut Here -

Mid-life is . . .   when you stop criticizing the older generation and start criticizing the younger one.

- Cut Here -

Mid-life is . . .   when your old classmates are so gray and wrinkled and bald they don't recognize you. *—Bennett Cerf*

- Cut Here -

Mid-life is . . .   when [you] are warned to slow down by a doctor instead of a police-man. *—Sidney Brody*

- Cut Here -

Mid-life is . . .   when you want to see how long your car will last instead of how fast it will go.

The Middlescence/Adolescence Stress Scales

On the life event scale on the left, record those events you have experienced during the past year by writing each score in the blank. If you have had an experience twice, double its point value. Add all the points and compare your results to the summary report at the bottom. Then on the life event scale on the right, record those events your adolescent has experienced during the last year (doubling those that have happened twice), and add up the score.

ADULTS

Life Event	Mean Value	
1. Death of spouse	100	____
2. Divorce	73	____
3. Marital separation	65	____
4. Jail term	63	____
5. Death of close family member	63	____
6. Personal injury or illness	53	____
7. Marriage	50	____
8. Fired from work	47	____
9. Marital reconciliation	45	____
10. Retirement	45	____
11. Change in health of family member	44	____
12. Pregnancy	40	____
13. Sex difficulties	39	____
14. Gain of new family member	39	____
15. Business readjustment	39	____
16. Change in financial state	38	____
17. Death of a close friend	37	____
18. Change to different line of work	36	____
19. Change in number of arguments with spouse	35	____
20. Major mortgage or debt	31	____
21. Foreclosure of mortgage or loan	30	____
22. Change in responsibilities at work	28	____
23. Son or daughter leaving home	30	____
24. Trouble with in-laws	29	____
25. Outstanding personal achievement	28	____
28. Wife begins or stops work	26	____
27. Begin or end school	26	____
28. Change in living conditions	25	____
29. Revision of personal habits	24	____
30. Trouble with boss	23	____
31. Change in work hours or conditions	20	____
32. Change in residence	20	____
33. Change in schools	20	____
34. Change in recreation	19	____
35. Change in church activities	19	____
36. Change in social activities	18	____
37. Minor mortgage or debt	17	____
38. Change in sleeping habits	16	____
39. Change in number of family get-togethers	15	____
40. Change in eating habits	15	____
41. Vacation	13	____
42. Christmas	12	____
43. Minor violations of the law	11	____
TOTAL		____

ADOLESCENTS

Life Event	Mean Value	
1. Death of family member	100	____
2. Divorce of parents	73	____
3. Breakup with long-term boy/girlfriend	45	____
4. Arrested	63	____
5. Death of a close friend	63	____
6. Personal injury or illness	53	____
7. Marriage	50	____
8. Flunks a school course	47	____
9. Makes up with old boy/girlfriend	35	____
10. Enters high school	45	____
11. Sustains serious sports injury	44	____
12. Pregnancy (self or girlfriend)	75	____
13. Becoming sexually active	50	____
14. Gain of new family member	29	____
15. Parent loses job	39	____
16. Major term paper due	38	____
17. Begins frequent drug or alcohol use	37	____
18. Loses part time job	36	____
19. Change in number of arguments with parents	35	____
20. Has auto accident	31	____
21. Flunks major test at school	30	____
22. Drops/adds school course	28	____
23. Brother or sister leaves home	30	____
24. Boy/girlfriend's parents dislike him/her	29	____
25. Outstanding personal achievement	28	____
26. Parent changes job	26	____
27. Begins or ends school	26	____
28. Change in living conditions	25	____
29. Change in personal habits	24	____
30. Trouble with teacher	23	____
31. Takes on extracurricular activity	20	____
32. Change in residence	20	____
33. Change in schools	40	____
34. Change in recreation	19	____
35. Change in church activities	19	____
38. Change in social activities	18	____
37. Gets grounded	17	____
38. Change in sleeping habits	16	____
39. Change in number of family get-togethers	15	____
40. Change in eating habits	15	____
41. Vacation	13	____
42. Christmas	12	____
43. Loses important piece of clothing	11	____
TOTAL		____

Using the Scale
0-150—no significant problems
150-199—Mild life crisis (33 percent chance of illness)
200-299—Moderate life crisis (50 percent chance of illness)
300 and over—Major life crisis (80 percent chance of illness)

J. H. Holmes and A. H. Rahe. "The Social Readjustment Rating Scale," *Journal of Psychosomatic Research* 1967, Volume 11, 213-318. © 1967 Pergamon Press, Ltd.

Using the Scale
0-150—no significant problems
150-199—Mild life crisis (33 percent chance of illness)
200-299—Moderate life crisis (50 percent chance of illness)
300 and over—Major life crisis (80 percent chance of illness)

The topics and values for the adolescents' scale are not based on scientific research. They simply demonstrate similar issues and stresses between teens and adults.

A Prayer of Hope

Complete steps one through five before turning the sheet upside down to follow the instructions for six through eleven.

1. Briefly describe in first person the primary way you and your teen (use his or her name) collide with each other or with similar life issues.

2. What one or two words best describe how this makes you feel?

3. What one or two words best describe how this makes your teen feel?

4. Describe briefly how you would like for you and your teen to help each other through this collision.

5. Imagine a worst-case scenario, and describe it in one or two sentences. That is, if the very worst outcome were to happen, what would it be?

As you follow these instructions, edit words as necessary to make your sentences flow as you write your prayer on a separate piece of paper. Make each step a new paragraph.

6. Near the top of a clean sheet of paper write the words, "Oh Lord," followed by your answer to question 1.

7. Write "I feel" followed by your answer to question 2.

8. Write "I'm sure [your teenager's name] feels" followed by your answer to question 3.

9. Write the words, "Please help us to" and then your answer to question 4.

10. Write the word, "Though," followed by your answer to question 5. Then follow that by the words from Psalm 27: 13, 14—"I am still confident of this: I will see the goodness of the Lord in the land of the living. Wait for the Lord; be strong and take heart and wait for the Lord."

11. Conclude your prayer with the words, "In Jesus' name, amen." Then sign your name.

Where I Thought I Was Going

Think back to when you first felt you had several real options for the direction your adult life would take. You may have changed goals several times since then, but sit back and let your mind return to that time as you answer the following questions. If there are some questions you cannot answer (if you did not have any goals in that area), that is okay.

1. About how old were you at this time? _____ What were you doing (working, going to college, getting married, etc.)?

2. To reorient you to that era, write a few descriptive words after the following statements.

    a. Biggest fad:

    b. My hair style:

    c. Most important world events:

    d. Most popular music:

    e. Most critical world concern:

    f. My relationship with my parents:

3. At that time, my goal spiritually was . . .

4. At that time, my vocational goal was . . .

5. At that time, my goal in terms of family was . . .

6. At that time, my goal personally was . . .

7. At that time, my goal physically was . . .

8. At that time, my goal for service to others was . . .

Living with Purpose

"Do you not know that in a race all the runners run, but only one gets the prize? Run in such a way as to get the prize. . . . Therefore I do not run like a man running aimlessly; I do not fight like a man beating the air" (I Cor. 9:24, 26).

In groups of three, read through Jesus' parable of the talents in Matthew 25:14-30. Then discuss and answer the following questions.

1. How would you describe the *purpose* governing the actions of the three servants to whom the master gave talents?

- Servant #1:

- Servant #2:

- Servant #3:

2. Who among the three had long-term goals? And who had short-term goals? Explain your answer.

3. What might have happened if the master had come back early before the one who had received five talents had time to see any return on his investment?

4. How do you think the risk he took reflects his purpose in life?

5. How would you apply Ephesians 5:15, 16 to each of these servants?

- Servant #1:

- Servant #2:

- Servant #3:

My Mission Statement

RS-2C

1. What are some of the characteristics that a "purpose in life" must have to make it worth-while and satisfying to the individual?

2. Consider your primary talents and abilities, your natural interests, the way you most easily relate to people, and the assets with which God has entrusted you (financial, where you live, the connections you have, family strengths, etc.). Your purpose in life should express all these things in order for your life to be abundant and full of meaning. Then, in each of the following areas, describe how you would like to be remembered and what you would like to have achieved before the end of your life. Test each statement with someone else to be sure it is a purpose and not a goal.

Spiritual

Vocational

Family

Personal

Physical

Service

3. After identifying your purpose in six areas, write a "Mission Statement" for your life. Ideally, it should encompass your purposes in scope, without necessarily repeating them.

Stepping-Stones

A longing fulfilled is sweet to the soul, but fools detest turning from evil. —Proverbs 13:19

To reach your full potential in life you must set goals. Select one long-term and one short-term goal in each area. Be sure your short-term goal is a direct stepping-stone for achieving the long-term goal.

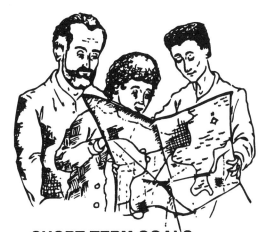

LONG-TERM GOALS

S P I R I T U A L	
V O C A T I O N A L	
F A M I L Y	
P E R S O N A L	
P H Y S I C A L	
S E R V I C E	

SHORT-TERM GOALS

S P I R I T U A L	
V O C A T I O N A L	
F A M I L Y	
P E R S O N A L	
P H Y S I C A L	
S E R V I C E	

Christmas Classics

RS-3A

A CHRISTMAS CAROL
by
Charles Dickens

Ebenezer Scrooge is a grasping, covetous man, the surviving partner in the firm of Scrooge and Marley. He is particularly stingy and cruel to his faithful office clerk, Bob Cratchit.

The night before Christmas, Scrooge has a dream in which he is visited by the miserable, chain-encumbered ghost of his old business partner, Jacob Marley. Marley, dead for seven years, tries to warn Scrooge to change his ways and make charity, mercy, and forbearance his business instead of accumulation.

After Marley departs, three spirits haunt Ebenezer Scrooge. The first is the Ghost of Christmas Past, who leads Scrooge on a tour of his youth, filled with much pain but also with moments of joy and opportunity, which Scrooge, unfortunately, did not embrace.

Next comes the Ghost of Christmas Present to show Scrooge how his miserly behavior has affected other people, especially the family of his clerk, Bob Cratchit, and his nephew, Fred. He learns how much people despise him. Scrooge is also shown the joy people can have when their attitude is generous and loving.

The third spirit is the Ghost of Christmas Yet to Come. It shows Scrooge his own gravestone in the cemetery. Scrooge is shocked that no one regrets his death; people plunder his possessions and then forget about him.

Scrooge finally awakens in the morning in his own bed to find that it is Christmas Day. He changes his ways, going about wishing everyone a Merry Christmas. He sends a huge turkey to the Cratchit home, contributes liberally to charity, goes to church, and then visits the home of his nephew for a Christmas party. The next day, he does everything possible to show appreciation and respect to Bob Cratchit.

To his surprise, Scrooge loves his new way of life.

IT'S A WONDERFUL LIFE
starring
Jimmy Stewart

George Bailey always wanted to do big things—build skyscrapers, airports—something to make a difference in the world. But by mid-life he thinks his chances have passed. Worse yet, the Bailey Building & Loan, to which he has given his life, seems doomed because of a mistake made by his bumbling Uncle Billy, who lost $8,000. (The misplaced money was actually found by ruthless Mr. Potter, who owns the bank and controls most of the town . . . except those homes and businesses supported by the benevolent Bailey Building & Loan.)

George, anticipating bankruptcy, scandal, and possibly prison, is so discouraged that he stumbles to the river to commit suicide.

Just then an angel, Clarence Oddbody, appears and tries to rescue George. Clarence succeeds temporarily by jumping into the river ahead of George, who rescues the angel rather than jump off the bridge himself.

But Clarence must still inspire the dejected George to want to live. George declares that it would have been better if he had never been born, and that gives Clarence an idea: Show George what the town of Bedford Falls would be like without him.

The deprived town is called Pottersville and is full of meanness. George's mother runs a shabby boardinghouse. The Bailey Park housing development is just an overgrown cemetery. George's wife, Mary Hatch, doesn't recognize him and suffers as a miserable spinster. His brother was no longer a famous war hero because he had died as a child when George wasn't there to rescue him from drowning. The nightmare continues until George appreciates his "wonderful life" and begs to return to it *as it was.*

When he returns, he finds that grateful townspeople have taken a collection to save the Bailey Building & Loan.

The Easy Yoke

Have one team member read Matthew 6:19-34, and then work through the following questions.

1. In order to enjoy an easy yoke in life, what distractions should we avoid (vss. 19, 25, 28, 31, 34)?

2. What priority should occupy the attention of the followers of Jesus? Why (vs. 20)?

3. Why does trying to store up treasure on earth increase our burden (vss. 19, 20, 27)?

4. What is the consequence of focusing on treasures on earth (vss. 21-23)?

5. What will be the experience of those who try to pursue conflicting priorities (vs. 24)?

6. What results does Jesus promise for those who heed these instructions (vs. 33)?

A Sample Plan

Select one of your "A" priority long-term goals from the previous resource sheet, "Stepping-Stones" (RS-2D), and develop the following plan for testing and accomplishing it.

My goal:

1. Is it accomplishable?

2. How is it related to my larger "purpose" in this area of life?

3. Does my goal pass the seven priority questions:
   - How urgent is it?
   - How important is it?
   - How often must it be done?
   - Can someone else do it?
   - Is it part of a larger purpose to which I am committed?
   - What will happen if it is not done at all?
   - Is it realistic?

4. What are the short-term goals (tasks) required to fulfill my long-term goal?

   _____

   _____

   _____

5. How will I measure the accomplishment of my short-term goals? (Include a "measurement" test for each short-term goal listed above. For example: *Goal*—Spend more one-on-one time with my teenager. *Measurement*—go out to breakfast on the weekend at least twice a month.)

   _____

   _____

   _____

6. Proverbs 15:22 says, "Plans fail for lack of counsel, but with many advisers they succeed." Who are three trusted advisers with whom I should test this goal?

   1. _____ , 2. _____ , 3. _____
   (If you are married, is one adviser your spouse?)

7. Proverbs 21:31 says, "The horse is made ready for the day of battle, but victory rests with the Lord." Who can be a prayer partner in helping me leave the "victory" of this plan in the Lord's hands? _____

Bring Back the Romance

Fact or Fiction?

For each of the following statements, indicate with an "X" on the scale from one to five how much you agree or disagree.

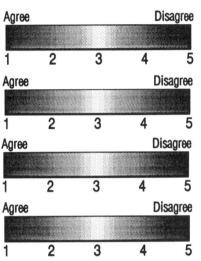

1. Men in their forties, as a rule, have less romantic or sexual responses than younger men.

Agree   Disagree
1   2   3   4   5

2. In our society today, those who experience a mid-life crisis almost certainly face the temptation to have an extramarital affair.

Agree   Disagree
1   2   3   4   5

3. Affairs are usually entered by married persons for physical gratification.

Agree   Disagree
1   2   3   4   5

4. The odds against divorce get better with each passing year of marriage.

Agree   Disagree
1   2   3   4   5

SUGGESTED BOOKS FOR MID-LIFE COUPLES

Augsburger, David. *Sustaining Love: Healing & Growth in the Passages of Marriage.* Ventura, Calif.: Regal Books, 1988.

Conway, Jim. *Men in Mid-Life Crisis.* Elgin, Ill.: David C. Cook Publishing Co., 1978.

Conway, Jim and Sally. *Women in Mid-Life Crisis.* Wheaton, Ill.: Tyndale House Publishers, Inc., 1983.

Jenkins, Jerry. *Loving Your Marriage Enough to Protect It.* Chicago: Moody Press, 1993.

Lush, Jean, with Vredevelt, Pam. *Women and Stress: A Practical Approach to Managing Tension.* Grand Rapids, Mich.: Revell, 1992.

Wright, H. Norman. *Seasons of a Marriage.* Ventura, Calif.: Regal Books, 1982.

Planting Hedges Around Your Marriage

- **Hedge No. 1**—Whenever I need to meet or dine or travel with an unrelated woman, I make it a threesome. Should an unavoidable last-minute complication make this impossible, my spouse hears it from me first.

- **Hedge No. 2**—I am careful about touching. While I might shake hands or squeeze an arm or a shoulder in greeting, I embrace only dear friends or relatives, and only in front of others.

- **Hedge No. 3**—If I pay a compliment to someone of the opposite sex, it is on clothes or hairstyle, not on the person herself/himself. Commenting on a nice outfit is much different than telling a woman that she herself looks pretty (or that a man looks handsome).

- **Hedge No. 4**—I avoid flirting or suggestive conversation, even in jest.

- **Hedge No. 5**—I remind my spouse often—verbally and in writing—that I remember my wedding vows: "Keeping you only unto me as long as we both shall live . . ."

- **Hedge No. 6**—From the time I or my spouse get home from work until the time the children go to bed, I do no writing or reading or office work. This gives me lots of time with the family and for my spouse and me to continue to court and date.

The Biblical Basis for Hedges

- When protective walls get broken down, even strong cities can become ruins. (See Psalm 89:40.)

- Job was richly blessed because God had a protective "hedge" around his life. (See Job 1:10.)

- Destructive sexual behavior begins with small indiscretions. (See Matthew 5:27, 28.)

- Temptation is a common experience, but giving in to it is not "inevitable." (See I Corinthians 10:13.)

- The best protection for my marriage relationship is to deliberately avoid temptation. (See II Timothy 2:22.)

- But if I have sinned in this area, the good news is that God's forgiveness enables me to start over. (See John 8:3-11.)

Adapted from *Loving Your Marriage Enough to Protect It*, by Jerry Jenkins. Copyright © 1989, 1993, Jerry Jenkins. Moody Press, Chicago, Illinois. Used by permission.

Striking the Match

The Romantic Husband

1. Find special ways to treat your wife in public. Say something nice about her when you introduce her. Seat her at dinner. Smile at her. Hold her coat when you're ready to go.
2. Keep yourself personally attractive and healthy. Your appearance does matter to her. Do what is necessary to avoid deserting her through an early death or disability.
3. Read some books related to family matters and child rearing, on spiritual growth and creativity. Discover ways to be more interesting, caring, and responsive to your wife.
4. What communicates love to your wife: flowers? small gifts? words of endearment? remembering anniversaries? asking her out for a date to do what she likes? Keep pursuing her even though you won her years ago.
5. Practice thoughtfulness. Keep her up-to-date with any changes in expectations ("I'll be a half-hour late getting home tonight"); bring her hot tea if she looks tired; help with chores before she asks; surprise her by doing jobs she usually expects to do.
6. Call her during the day to tell her you can hardly wait to see her. Be willing to talk about your intimate times together. Ask her what you can do to make them better.
7. Never criticize her in public, point out something she cannot change, or compare her unfavorably with other women.
8. Never lay a hand on her or the children except in love.
9. Genuinely appreciate your wife for who she is. Don't try to change her. Instead, give praise and affirmation.
10. Make the sacrifices necessary which will allow time for you and your wife to be together. Love takes time.

—————————————————— Cut Here ——————————————————✂

The Romantic Wife

1. Keep yourself personally attractive and healthy. Your husband will take it as a personal compliment that you are taking care of yourself "for him."
2. How does your husband like to spend leisure time and weekends? Can you come up with creative compromises so that his needs and your needs can both be met?
3. Read some good books; share them with your husband and discuss the ideas together.
4. Listen. Be a good sounding board. Take an interest in things that interest your husband. Be ready to share his excitement—or disappointments.
5. Welcome his romantic advances.
6. Become actively involved in lovemaking. Your husband's positive feelings about himself and your romance depend a lot on your active participation.
7. Be loyal to your husband. Never criticize him, put him on the spot, or make him feel foolish in front of others.
8. Appreciate your husband for who he is; focus on his strengths, not his shortcomings. Give him genuine compliments at every opportunity. Reassure him of his masculinity.
9. Don't try to change your husband through nagging or attack; it breeds hostility or counterattack. We can change only ourselves; others tend to change in response to us.
10. A husband and wife need time together enjoying life and sharing. Let some of the chores go for cuddling time in front of the TV; plan some creative "dates"; exercise together; go out for coffee and talk.

An Asset Checklist for Teens and Parents

If you have more than one teenager, fill out one sheet for each teen.

How many external assets are present in your teen's life?

___ Parents are loving, easy to talk to, and available when teens want to talk.

___ Parents frequently take time to talk seriously with their children.

___ Parents express their own standards for teenage behavior.

___ Parents talk with their teenager about school and sometimes help with school work and attend school events.

___ Parents set rules and enforce the consequences when the rules are broken.

___ Parents check on where their teenager is going, with whom, and for how long.

___ Parents are approachable when the teenager has something serious to talk about.

___ The number of nights the teenager may spend out of the home "for fun and recreation" is limited.

___ The teenager has three or more adults, in addition to parents, to whom he or she could go for help.

___ The teenager has frequent serious conversations with an adult who is not his or her own parent.

___ The teenager's friends are a constructive influence, are doing well at school, are staying away from contact with drugs, alcohol and other at-risk behavior.

___ The teenager attends church at least once a month.

___ The teenager sees the school atmosphere as caring and encouraging.

___ The teenager participates in band or orchestra or takes lessons on a musical instrument involving three or more hours of practice a week.

___ The teenager participates in school sports activities or other organizations three or more hours per week.

___ The teenager participates in non-school-sponsored sports or other organizations three or more hours per week.

How many internal assets are present in your teen's life?

___ Tries to do his or her best at school.

___ Hopes to be educated beyond high school.

___ Earns above-average school grades.

___ Does six or more hours of homework weekly.

___ Is good at making friends.

___ Tries to stand up for his or her beliefs.

___ Cares about others' feelings.

___ Is good at planning ahead.

___ Is good at making decisions.

___ Has a positive attitude toward self.

___ Envisions a happy future for herself or himself.

___ Shows concern for the poor.

___ Is interested in helping and improving life for others.

___ Holds values that prohibit having sex as a teenager.

___ Total number checked.

Peter L. Benson, "The Troubled Journey: A Profile of American Youth" (Minneapolis: Lutheran Brotherhood), 1990. Reprinted by permission of the Lutheran Brotherhood.

Patterns of a Strong Family, Building a Firm Base

1. Members of strong families express appreciation to each other very often.

2. Strong families spend a lot of time together. As a matter of fact, they intentionally cut down on the number of outside activities and involvements in order to minimize fragmentation of their family life.

3. Strong families work hard at keeping lines of communication open and keeping their communication as positive as possible.

4. Strong families are devout. They are active in a church as a family; and beyond that, they regularly read the Bible and pray together. But most importantly, they have a constant sense that God cares and is involved in the daily processes of their lives.

5. Strong families are committed to the family, to spending time together, and to making each other happy.

Based on research done at Oklahoma State University. Reported in *Family Strength Magazine*, Fall 1976, 6-8.

Mutual Support/Decisive Living

1. What practical ways of mutual support have we worked on or experienced in our family?
2. What practical ways of decisive living have we worked on or experienced in our family?

Mutual Support	Decisive Living

The Good, the Bad, and the Ugly

Imagine a "shootout" you had with your parents when you were a teenager. Let yourself concentrate on it for several moments. How did it start? What happened? How did it end? When you have fully recalled the situation, answer the following questions.

1. Describe what the conflict was about.

2. How did your parents deal with conflict?

3. How did you deal with the conflict?

4. James 4:1 asks, "What causes fights and quarrels among you? Don't they come from your desires that battle within you?" Conflicts are seldom about such surface things as clothes, hair, or curfews, but about deeper goals within: the desire to be accepted by one's peers, to feel grown up, etc. When the true goals are disclosed (both those of the parent and the teen), it is easier to move toward a resolution.

What was your underlying goal in the conflict?

What was your parents' deeper goal?

5. Describe what you learned about conflict from your experience as an adolescent by completing the sentence, "Conflict is . . ." (For instance, "Conflict is useful because . . ." or ". . . bad because . . ." or ". . . pointless because. . . .")

Conflict is . . .

6. If you ever benefited by conflict (such as getting a later curfew), describe what it was and how you achieved it.

Ways to Deal with Conflict

Which Way Is Best?

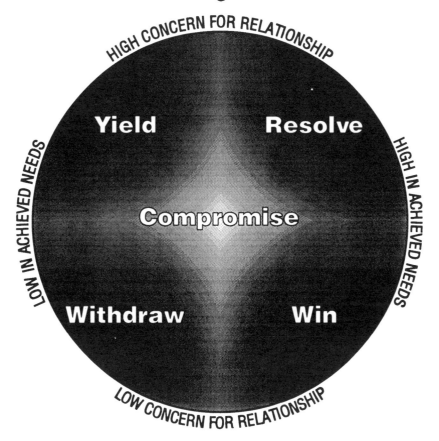

HIGH CONCERN FOR RELATIONSHIP

HIGH IN ACHIEVED NEEDS

LOW IN ACHIEVED NEEDS

Yield

Resolve

Compromise

Withdraw

Win

LOW CONCERN FOR RELATIONSHIP

- **Withdraw** has the lowest value because the person gives up both achieving goals and fostering the relationship. However, if this style is used only temporarily as a cooling-off step, it can be beneficial.
- **Win** may achieve a goal but can sacrifice the relationship. In a family, personal relationships should be more important than any goal other than direct obedience to God.
- **Yield** maintains the relationship but sacrifices the goals. However, in the long run, too frequent yielding can damage the relationship because it destroys respect.
- **Compromise** attempts to work out some needs, but the bargaining involved may mean that you compromise some of your goals.
- **Resolve** is the most desirable style because it strengthens relationships as you seek to meet personal needs.

Adapted from James G. T. Fairchild, *When You Don't Agree: A Guide to Resolving Marriage and Family Conflicts* (Scottdale, Penn.: Herald Press, 1977), 19.

Ways to "Win" In Which Everyone Loses

Silenced by Shaming: "Your mother and I work very hard to provide you everything you need and most of what you want. Do you think it's easy? Do you think we get everything we want?"

Silenced by Blackmailing: "It would break my heart if I thought. . . . It's very hard for a mother to see her baby growing away from her."

Silenced by Overpowering: "You will listen to me respectfully and you will talk to me respectfully. Is that understood?"

Handling Conflict
The ASRAC Way

"Finally, all of you, live in harmony with one another; be sympathetic, love as brothers, be compassionate and humble. Do not repay evil with evil or insult with insult, but with blessing, because to this you were called so that you may inherit a blessing" (I Peter 3:8, 9).

"A gentle answer turns away wrath, but a harsh word stirs up anger" (Proverbs 15:1).

Share concern by finding points you can authentically agree upon.

Accept your teen's resentment without making a defense of any kind. This does not mean that you agree with your teen, but that he or she has a right to his or her feelings.

Reflect your teen's emotions by putting them into your own words to demonstrate your understanding.

Confirm that the conflict is truly over when agreement is reached. (Pray together and exchange hugs, etc.)

Advocate a resolution/ solution that will end the conflict with "logical" reason for accepting it.

Charles Bradshaw, *You and Your Teen* (Elgin, Ill.: David C. Cook Publishing Co., 1981), 67.

Top Influences on Teens

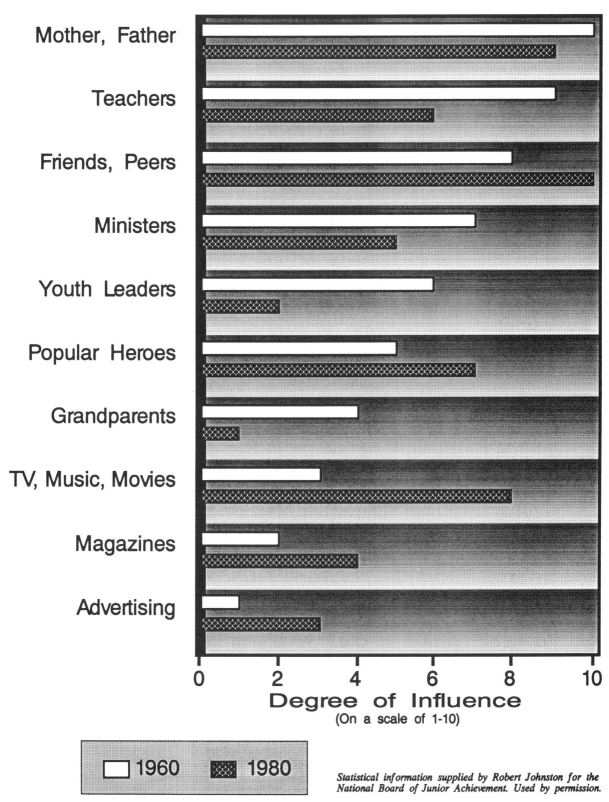

Degree of Influence
(On a scale of 1-10)

1960 1980

Statistical information supplied by Robert Johnston for the National Board of Junior Achievement. Used by permission.

Moral Behavior

In James 4:17 we read, "Anyone, then, who knows the good he ought to do and doesn't do it, sins." This passage suggests that moral behavior has two basic components: *Knowledge* of good and evil and then the *Will* to do what is right—the active choice of good over evil.

KNOWLEDGE

Jesus suggests that we will be judged partially according to the light we have received—our knowledge of good and evil: "From the one who has been entrusted with much, much more will be asked" (Luke 12:48b). However, accountability begins at a more basic level. In Romans 1:18-20, Paul says that even those who don't know Scripture are without excuse because they can observe enough in nature to know of God's existence and a distinction between good and evil.

Knowledge comes to us in three ways: Experience, Example, and Instruction.

1. Experience

Golden Rule

At a very early age, children experience the difference between good and evil. Love, comfort, and security start to create the category of good. Anger, pain, and fear begin the notion of bad. The appeal to do unto others as we would have them do unto us is based on this most basic principle. Everyone can understand it.

2. Example

The good parent offers a model to the child that expands the child's moral sensitivity. But the ability to identify inconsistencies in parental behavior is greater in teens. The teen will experience disappointment and possibly anger in finding that his or her model is not perfect. So we must seek God's help to do our best. Biblical characters are models, and Christ, Himself, invites us: "Learn from me, for I am gentle and humble in heart" (Matt. 11:29). Certainly, He is the only model without disappointment. →Christ

3. Instruction

Our knowledge of good and evil also expands through instruction, which is frequently accompanied by explanation and dialogue. The Apostle Paul employed this approach in presenting the Gospel and in teaching right living. Teens are mature enough to appreciate this, but they will need a convincing case.

When this is not possible, we can explain that there are times when we, too, must accept something as right or wrong on the authority of the source.

WILL

Knowing the difference between good and evil is of no value until we act on that knowledge. Some choices in life are extremely complex with uncertainty about what is truly right and perhaps with strong pressures to act one way or the other. And yet we all choose. How we choose is influenced by three elements: Consequences, Attitudes, and Grace.

1. Consequences

There are two components of consequences: *rewards* and *punishments*. It may be a surprise to the modern thinking person, but God never seems to apologize for informing us of the consequences in His attempt to encourage us to choose what is right. Consequences are reality, and only the fool ignores them.

2. Attitudes   *What motivates us?*

Another influence on our will—the way we choose—is our attitudes, particularly those of *love, hate* and *indifference*. Our love for another person can motivate us. Our love for God and God's righteousness (ultimate good) can motivate us. Jesus said, "If you love me, you will obey what I command" (John 14:15).

It is also possible to be motivated by hate, but indifference may be the most dangerous attitude. There can be the illusion of doing nothing wrong, but when it comes to moral behavior, to fail to decide is to decide.

In our uniquely human way, we can choose for our attitudes to override the consequences. There are many examples of heroic deeds or unselfish acts done in the face of dire consequences, so we are not driven by consequences.

3. Grace

With all the evil in the world, it is easy to feel that our children do not have a chance. But God has tipped the scale toward good. He has primed our attitudes toward good by His love. "We love because he first loved us" (I John 4:19). He offers forgiveness and salvation. This is the grace of God that draws us to Him.

In the Thick of It

Jill

You are sixteen and want to go on a weekend ski trip with friends. Your main interest is your boyfriend, Bob. There will be about a dozen in the group, and you will be staying in a cabin leased by the parents of one of the kids. No adults will be present. You and Bob have been over-involved physically (without your parents' knowledge), but you hope to cool things down—if you can hold Bob off. He teases you a lot about your old-fashioned hang-ups. He's not a Christian, and he really isn't the kind of guy you'd want to marry, but he's a lot of fun for now. You begin the roleplay by asking to go.

— — — — — — — — — — — — — Fold and tear here — — — — — — — — — — — — — — — —

Father

Your sixteen-year-old, Jill, has been dating more than you'd like for a girl her age. She seems to be getting too serious about a guy you've met only once. You didn't like him very well. He seemed flippant when you asked him what he liked most in school. You want Jill to go to college and marry a good Christian. She doesn't seem serious about God or her studies lately.

— — — — — — — — — — — — — Fold and tear here — — — — — — — — — — — — — — — —

Mother

You're very worried about the relationship your sixteen-year-old, Jill, is having with Bob. You know he's not a Christian, and Jill has been increasingly elusive about sharing with you. Once, you happened to walk into the living room when Jill and Bob were in an intimate embrace. Later, she wouldn't talk about it. You remember with some embarrassment how overwhelming the physical side of things was when you were a teenager.

— — — — — — — — — — — — — Fold and tear here — — — — — — — — — — — — — — — —

Questions:

1. How is *experience* by the teen relevant to acquiring knowledge in this area?
2. How can parents employ *example* to further the teen's knowledge of good and evil?
3. What type of *instruction* might teens be most likely to accept on this issue?
4. How should parents relate *consequences* to this issue?
5. How can the teen's *attitudes* be most positively encouraged in this situation?

Adolescence Is . . .

RS-8A

------------------------------ Cut here ------------------------------ ✂

God made babies so precious and adorable that we don't mind getting up at 3:00 A.M. to feed them . . . and He made adolescents so obnoxious that we don't mind when they leave home!

—*anonymous*

------------------------------ Cut here ------------------------------

An adolescent is a two-year-old with hormones and wheels.

—*Foster Cline, child psychiatrist*

------------------------------ Cut here ------------------------------

Adolescence is that period when children feel that their parents should be told the facts of life.

—*anonymous*

------------------------------ Cut here ------------------------------

Most teenagers think that their family circle is composed of squares.

—*Dan Bennett*

------------------------------ Cut here ------------------------------

A teenager is a person who gets up on a Saturday morning and has nothing to do, and by bedtime has it only half done.

—*Rough Notes magazine*

------------------------------ Cut here ------------------------------

Developmental Tasks of Teenagers

RS-8B

1. **PHYSICAL—Accepting one's changing body and adjusting to physical maturity:**

   - Coming to terms with the new size, shape, function, and potential of one's maturing body.
   - Accepting differences between one's own physique and the body build of others.
   - Accepting one's own physique rather than an unrealistic "ideal."
   - Understanding what the changes at puberty mean and anticipating maturity as a man or woman in a wholesome way.

2. **SEX ROLES—Achieving a satisfying and socially accepted masculine or feminine role:**

   - Developing new and more mature relationships with peer groups of both sexes.
   - Learning what it means to be male or female in one's culture.
   - Becoming acceptable as a member of one or more groups of peers.
   - Learning to relate in positive ways with members of the opposite sex, and becoming comfortable in dating situations.

3. **VOCATIONAL—Selecting and preparing for an occupation and economic independence:**

   - Choosing an occupation in line with interests, abilities, and opportunities.
   - Preparing oneself through schooling, specialized training, and personal responsibility to obtain and hold a position.
   - Seeking tryout or apprenticeship experiences wherever possible along the lines of future vocational interests.

4. **SOCIAL—Establishing one's identity as a socially responsible person:**

   - Developing a mature set of values and ethical controls appropriate to one's culture.
   - Implementing worthy standards in one's life.

5. **EMOTIONAL—Achieving emotional independence from parents and other adults:**

   - Becoming free of childish dependence upon one's parents.
   - Learning how to be an autonomous person who is capable of making decisions and running his or her own life.

Adapted from Charles Bradshaw, *You and Your Teen* (Elgin, Ill.: David C. Cook Publishing Co., 1985), 36-37.

Three Parents

Father—Prodigal (Luke 15:11-32)	King David—Absalom (II Samuel 11; 13-15; 18)	Me—My Teen
1. "Adolescent" Problem	1. "Adolescent" Problem Compare II Samuel 11 with 13 (esp. vss. 22, 32).	1. Adolescent Problem
2. How Parent Responded to Problem	2. How Parent Responded to Problem II Samuel 13 (esp. vs. 21).	2. My Response to Problem
3. Attitude of Parent During Rebellion	3. Attitude of Parent During Rebellion II Samuel 13 (esp. vs. 37, 39), 15 (esp. vss. 13, 14).	3. My Attitude During Teen's Rebellion
4. How Parent's Love Was Expressed	4. How Parent's Love Was Expressed II Samuel 13:37-39; 14:21-33.	4. How I Express Love in Hard Times
5. Parent's Attitude When Child Returned	5. Parent's Attitude When Child Returned II Samuel 14:21-28.	5. My Attitude When Child "Returns" to Me
6. End Result	6. End Result II Samuel 15:10-12; 18:9, 14, 15, 32, 33.	6. End Result

General Guidelines For Letting Go

As with the prodigal son, our children may leave home before we think they are ready. However, if we are wise, there are ways we can prepare them to make it on their own.

1. Loosen, don't tighten, the controls as children grow.

2. Encourage and reward, instead of discouraging, their growing independence by increasing their responsibilities and privileges year by year. The more we encourage and allow their independence, the less they will have to prove it by rebelling.

3. Teach them how to think, not what to think. Allow them to make decisions and to fail. Encourage them to become problem solvers.

4. Don't regularly do anything for them that they are capable of doing for themselves.

5. Recognize and nurture their individuality. They are unique personalities, not our clones. They are gifts, not possessions. We raise them to serve God, not us.

6. Keep our goals in mind. Like a mountain climber striving to reach the summit, we must keep our eyes focused on our goals and not on the thorny bushes and slippery rocks that discourage and impede our progress along the way. We raise our children to leave us. Our responsibility is to equip and to prepare them for life without us. Their success is our success.

Taken from the book, *LEARNING TO LET GO* by Carol Kuykendall, 21. Copyright © 1985 by Carol Kuykendall. Used by permission of Zondervan Publishing House.

Teens vs. Parents

Instructions: Make two copies of this resource sheet. Cut apart the sections as indicated so that "parent" and "teen" roles each have a copy.

— — — — — — — — — — — — — — Cut here — — — — — — — — — — — — — — — ✂

Section A

TEEN: (giving "the look") Go bowling with the family? You've got to be kidding! This is Friday night—I've been looking forward to doing something with my friends all week! Besides, I'm getting too old for this "family night" stuff.

PARENT: But you went ice-skating with Chris's folks just last week.

TEEN: That's different! The Jensens are cool. All the kids like to hang out at their house. But no way am I going to go bowling with my bratty sister! And you can't make me!

— — — — — — — — — — — — — — Cut here — — — — — — — — — — — — — —

Section B

PARENT: What do you mean, the party isn't over until one o'clock? Your curfew is twelve, young lady, and not a minute later!

TEEN: (wailing) But, Dad! If I have to be home by twelve, that means someone else has to leave the party early to bring me home. I'm the only one among my friends who has to be home so early. Why do you always have to ruin my fun?

PARENT: Fun? You don't have to stay out all night to have fun. The later the party, the more you're asking for trouble.

TEEN: Why do you always assume the worst? You don't trust me!

— — — — — — — — — — — — — — Cut here — — — — — — — — — — — — — —

Section C

TEEN: Church is boring. I don't want to go anymore.

PARENT: But you became a member just last year. Church is important.

TEEN: So? There's no one my age. All we do is get preached at and made to feel guilty about everything. At least let me go to Sammie's church on Sunday. He says they've got a neat youth group over there.

PARENT: You don't know anything about that church. Forget it. We attend church as a family.

Barriers and Builders

BARRIERS	BUILDERS
1. ASSUMING: Thinking you know what your teen thinks, what he or she will do, and how he or she will respond. *("I knew you wouldn't be interested so I didn't tell you"; "Don't forget to pack a toothbrush"; You always get upset when . . .")*	1. CHECKING: Asking your teen what he or she thinks, what he or she plans to do, or trying to understand why your teen chose to respond the way he or she did. *("What do you need for your overnight?")*
2. RESCUING/EXPLAINING: Rescuing your teen so he or she doesn't learn from the consequences of his or her choices. Stepping in to explain what happened rather than asking the kind of questions that will help a teen discover what happened. *("If you don't _____, this is what will happen"; or, "This is why it happened, and this is what you better do to fix it.")*	2. EXPLORING: Asking the "What? Why? and How?" questions to help your teen become aware of his or her own perceptions and the consequences of his or her choices. *("Does this purchase leave you enough money for the other things you need before your next paycheck?")*
3. DIRECTING: Giving instructions on each step to make sure it's done the "right" way (i.e, my way). Controlling the situation and the other people in it. *("Line up the bowls in this corner, dirty plates here, cups in this rack . . ." vs. "Please load the dishwasher.")*	3. ENCOURAGING/INVITING: Seeing teens as assets rather than objects or recipients. Allowing for mistakes and different ways of doing things. *("I'm going to be late today. I'd appreciate it if you would get supper on the table—your choice.")*
4. EXPECTING: Setting high standards and then pointing out the person's failure to reach those standards. *(Parent: "I thought I told you to clean the bathroom." Teen: "I did!" Parent: "I can still see dirt under the radiator.")*	4. CELEBRATING: Recognizing progress and encouraging any step in that direction. *("I sure appreciate bathing in a clean tub!" At a later time: "Here's an old toothbrush—it's helpful for cleaning the grout.")*
5. ADULTISMS: Adultisms presume your teen can read your mind and think as you do. *("How come you never . . . ?" "Why can't you ever . . . ?" "Don't you realize?" "How many times do I have to tell you?")*	5. RESPECT: Being willing to look at issues from your teen's perspective. The language of respect is, "What is your understanding of _____?" and "Let me be sure I understand what you think (or feel)." *("What was your understanding of when you needed to be home to fix supper?")*

Adapted from H. Stephen Glenn and Jane Nelsen, *Raising Self-Reliant Children in a Self-Indulgent World* (Rocklin, Calif.: Prima Publishing and Communications, 1989), 72-93. Used by permission.

Freedoms Earned Through Responsibility

Responsibilities	Freedoms
Early Adolescence • Do own laundry, occasional meal preparation, yard work, limited car maintenance.	• Use of money, decide when to go to bed, menu selection, clothing allowance.
Middle Adolescence • Regular menu and meal preparation, pay for own clothes, learn about family budget system, more car maintenance.	• Use of family car, generous weekend curfews, a part-time job.
Late Adolescence • Home remodeling projects, major car maintenance, help with family finances (car insurance, etc.).	• Own car, curfew dropped, "inform" parents of whereabouts rather than ask permission,* out-of-town trips.

* Parents do have the right—and responsibility—to set broad moral limits for anyone living under their roof, but older teens should not have to get permission for otherwise acceptable activities.

Chart adapted from *TEEN SHAPING* by Len Kageler, 147. Copyright © 1990 by Leonard M. Kageler. Used by permission of Fleming H. Revell Company, a division of Baker Book House, Grand Rapids, Mich.

Responsibilities	Freedoms
Early Adolescence •	•
Middle Adolescence •	•
Late Adolescence •	•

Parents Are People, Too

Cultivate My Personal Identity

Parents often get entangled in the emotions, achievements, and problems of their children. It's important to nurture your sense of self—that you are an individual apart from your children. To do this, you must have time alone to help you keep in touch with "who you are."

List two or three ways you can cultivate your personal identity.

Cultivate Other Relationships

Any relationship takes time to nurture and develop. That includes your relationship with God, with your spouse—both of which take priority over your relationship with your children—as well as with friends.

List two or three ways you can cultivate your relationships.

Cultivate Outside Interests

If you work outside the home, "outside interests" may already seem built into your life, competing with parenthood. But it's important to nurture personal interests, develop neglected talents, even explore new job possibilities, both to help keep alive your personal identity in the midst of parenting demands, and to provide meaningful involvements when children finally leave home.

List two or three ways you can cultivate outside interests.

Setting Limits

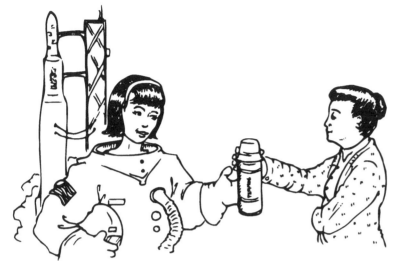

As you prepare your teen for launching . . .

1. Recognize that every teenager is different.

2. Discuss the possible limits with your teenager before making a decision.

3. Differentiate between a biblical absolute and your personal preference.

4. Be flexible.

5. Compare your standards to those of a variety of other parents.

6. Work toward cooperative development of standards.

7. Allow increased freedom and responsibility with age.

8. Never set a limit without giving a good reason.

Bruce Narramore, *Adolescence Is Not an Illness* (Old Tappan, N.J.: Fleming H. Revell Co., 1980).

Blueprint for Building Self-Esteem

RS-10B

My teen's name_____

Area of strongest self-esteem_____

Area of weakest self-esteem_____

WEEK ONE

-
-
-

WEEK TWO

-
-
-

WEEK THREE

-
-
-

Recommended Books to Read:

Glenn, H. Stephen, and Nelsen, Jane. *Raising Self-Reliant Children in a Self-Indulgent World*. New York: St. Martin's Press, 1989.

Kageler, Len. *Teen Shaping—Solving the Discipline Dilemma: What Works, What Doesn't*. Old Tappan, N. J.: Fleming H. Revell Co., 1990.

Kuykendall, Carol. *Learning to Let Go*. Grand Rapids, Mich.: Zondervan Publishing House, 1985.

Laurent, Robert. *Bringing Your Teen Back to God*. Elgin, Ill.: David C. Cook Publishing Co., 1991.

_____. *Keeping Your Teen in Touch with God*. Elgin, Ill.: David C. Cook Publishing Co., 1991.

Narramore, Bruce. *Adolescence Is Not an Illness*. Old Tappan, N. J.: Fleming H. Revell Co., 1980.

Are You over the Hill?

- Total Face-lifts in U.S., 1990: 48,743
  (91 percent were women) . . .
  percentage aged thirty-five to fifty: 27
  percentage aged fifty-one to sixty-four: 58

- Total tummy tucks in U.S., 1990: 20,213
  (93 percent were women) . . .
  percentage aged thirty-five to fifty: 64
  percentage aged fifty-one to sixty-four: 15

- Total hair transplants in U.S., 1990: 3,188
  (100 percent were men) . . .
  percentage aged thirty-five to fifty: 64
  percentage aged fifty-one to sixty-four: 15

- Median age of an American using hair-color product . . .
  women: 43.14
  men: 43.02

Source: American Society of Plastic and Reconstructive
Surgeons, Simmon, 1992, as reported in *Newsweek*,
Dec. 7, 1992, 54.

Do you agree or disagree with the following statements:

		True	False
1.	The overall health of a person in his or her forties sharply declines.	❏	❏
2.	The years of greatest productivity in various professions are between twenty-eight and thirty-two.	❏	❏
3.	A person can learn anything more quickly during the early twenties than at any other time of life.	❏	❏
4.	A person's greatest physical strength is experienced in one's twenties.	❏	❏
5.	The average person's physical appearance changes in mid-life.	❏	❏

Coming to Terms with Mid-Life

Rate how satisfied you are with the following areas of your life. For every question, enter a number (0—3) in the blank on the left for how you feel today. Then in the blank to the right, enter another number (0—3) to show whether you felt less satisfied, the same, or more satisfied five to seven years ago. (The section on work is meant for everyone, including career homemakers.)

0 = DOES NOT APPLY	DIDN'T APPLY = 0
1 = NOT SATISFIED	FELT LESS SATISFIED = 1
2 = SOMEWHAT SATISFIED	FELT THE SAME = 2
3 = VERY SATISFIED	FELT MORE SATISFIED = 3

TODAY   5 TO 7 YEARS AGO

____ a. **MY MARRIAGE IN GENERAL** . . . . ____
____ b. My spouse as a person . . . . ____
____ c. How well we communicate . . . . ____
____ d. How well we handle money . . . . ____
____ e. How much time we spend together . . . . ____
____ f. Sexual relationship with my spouse . . . . ____
____ g. Our level of status and/or prestige . . . . ____
____ h. Our common interests . . . . ____
____ i. Our common values . . . . ____
____ j. Our shared spiritual values . . . . ____
____ k. Our future together . . . . ____

____ l. **BEING A PARENT** . . . . ____
____ m. My relationship with my young children . . . . ____
____ n. My relationship with my teenage children . . ____
____ o. My relationship with my grown children . . . . ____
____ p. My spouse's relationship with our children . ____
____ q. How much I give my children of myself, etc. ____
____ r. The people my children are becoming . . . . . ____

____ s. **MY WORK IN GENERAL** . . . . ____
____ t. The challenge of my work . . . . ____
____ u. How fulfilling my work is . . . . ____
____ v. How well I do my work . . . . ____
____ w. What I've accomplished . . . . ____
____ x. How far I have advanced . . . . ____
____ y. The prestige I feel I have . . . . ____
____ z. My income and/or standard of living . . . . . . ____
____ aa. My future in this work . . . . ____

____ bb. **MY OUTSIDE INTERESTS** . . . . ____
____ cc. My friendships . . . . ____
____ dd. The amount of my leisure time . . . . ____
____ ee. My church involvement . . . . ____
____ ff. My community involvement . . . . ____
____ gg. My hobbies . . . . ____
____ hh. The amount I give of myself to others . . . . . ____

____ ii. **MY OVERALL SELF-IMAGE** . . . . ____
____ jj. My physical appearance . . . . ____
____ kk. My spouse's appearance . . . . ____
____ ll. Thinking about my age . . . . ____
____ mm. My athletic ability . . . . ____
____ nn. How our home looks to others . . . . ____
____ oo. How well people like me . . . . ____
____ pp. My spiritual growth . . . . ____
____ qq. My goals/dreams . . . . ____

Among your responses on the scale to the left, with which two are you most satisfied?

Place letters here: _____   _____

With which two are you least satisfied?

Place letters here: _____   _____

For the two least satisfying areas, describe what you think needs to change in terms of what can be altered or what you need to accept.

1.

2.

Adapted from "Is Your Marriage Better Than It Was Five Years Ago?" *MARRIAGE PARTNERSHIP* magazine (Spring/1990), 42. Copyright © 1990, published by Christianity Today, Inc., Carol Stream, Illinois. Used by Permission.

My Parents' Situation

Write a sentence or two for each category describing your parents' current status in that area. Begin with your biological parents (if they are living); substitute in-laws or other older relatives for whom you feel responsible where there are gaps.

1. Living Situation
    a.

    b.

2. Physical Health
    a.

    b.

3. Mental Health
    a.

    b.

4. Emotional Health
    a.

    b.

5. Work/Interests/Involvements
    a.

    b.

6. Relationship with Me
    a.

    b.

Role Reversal

Role Reversal

Instructions for the Aging Parent

You know you have been getting more forgetful lately, and it's embarrassing to be asked if you have done the most elementary things. Sometimes you say yes even when you haven't, because you don't want to admit you need help.

Everyone seems to be hurrying you all the time and won't let you figure things out or just enjoy life. It makes you feel like you are being treated like a child. You resent that and snap back.

The scene begins in the grocery store where your adult children have taken you after Sunday dinner so you can pick up a few things.

— — — — — — — — — — — — — — — — — Cut here — — — — — — — — — — — — — — — — — ✂

Role Reversal

Instructions for the Adult Children

It's Sunday afternoon, and you are taking Mom (Dad) home after dinner. She (he) just wanted to stop at the grocery store to pick up a few things—to save a trip later. She (he) is having trouble deciding whether to get Cheerios or Honey Nut Cheerios. She (he) seems to dawdle forever with things these days.

Maybe she (he) is concerned about money. You ask if she (he) has balanced her (his) checkbook recently. However, last time she (he) said yes, it later turned out to be no.

Then you wonder if she (he) is feeling especially exhausted because she (he) forgot to take her (his) medication after dinner. Lately, you have to check up on everything. You wonder sometimes about Alzheimer's; it's as though she (he) is a kid and you must be the parent.

It's getting late and you've got to get home.

Where Will They Live?

RS-12C

Where Will They Live?

Instructions for the Aging Parent

You know that it is harder to get things done around the house lately. The porch needs repairing and the rugs need shampooing. You'll get to it when you can. It would sure be easier if one of your children would volunteer to come over and help more often.

Lately, they have been talking about moving you to a retirement center. You don't want to go. It seems like the beginning of the end to you—all those old people, somebody dying every week. Besides, you'd be so far from your friends, your familiar corner store, and . . . you couldn't take your little dog. Old as Puff is, he's your best companion. You couldn't possibly give him up. Who would take him?

If you must move, why don't the kids let you move in with them? You could be helpful, and they've got extra room.

– – – – – – – – – – – – – – – – – – Cut here – – – – – – – – – – – – – – – – – – ✂

Where Will They Live?

Instructions for the Adult Children

Mom (Dad) just isn't making it alone these days. The house smells, there are needed repairs everywhere, and you are afraid she (he) will have a heart attack or get hurt one of these days. You think she (he) ought to move into a nice retirement center you have found. It's affordable; she'd (he'd) be with people her (his) own age where she'd (he'd) have more in common. And she'd (he'd) get regular, nutritious meals.

You bring up the idea again, this time determined to convince her (him) to make the decision.

When One Parent Dies

RS-12D

When One Parent Dies

Instructions for the Aging Parent

Your spouse died a year ago. You feel that you have gotten over the initial grief. It was not unexpected, and it was not an unusually painful death. It was what you and your spouse had both hoped for in terms of living a full life and not lingering. However, you never realized the loneliness would be so severe. Your other wish had been that you would go together.

But you must get on with life.

You are especially concerned about your children, however. You don't think they have dealt with their grief, primarily because they have not fully faced their loss. They've kept themselves so busy, there was no time to think. Could it be that death reminds them too much that they are no longer so young? Or that you may die soon, too?

You start the conversation by trying to raise the issue with them.

— Cut here — ✂

When One Parent Dies

Instructions for the Adult Children

Dad (Mom) died nearly a year ago. There was so much to do after his (her) death that you hardly had time to think about his (her) passing once the funeral was over. Of course, you all cried there.

But then you had to resettle Mom (Dad), sell the old house, and dispose of all the accumulated things of a lifetime. Life's been a whirlwind since then.

You think Mom (Dad) is getting along fine, but she (he) always wants to talk about Dad's (Mom's) death. You know you should let her (him) remember him (her) in whatever way she (he) wants, but you'd rather not be the audience. It makes you feel funny.

Biography Game

7

At age seven, his family was forced out of their home because of a legal technicality. He had to go to work to help support them. At age nine, while he was still a backward, shy little boy, his mother died.

49

At age forty-nine, he ran for the Senate again—and lost again. At age fifty-one, he was elected president of the United States.

45

At age at forty-five, he ran for the Senate and lost. Two years later, he was defeated for vice president nomination.

41

At age forty-one, adding heartache to an already unhappy marriage, his four-year-old son died. The next year he was rejected for land officer.

22

At age twenty-two, he lost his job as a store clerk. He wanted to go to law school, but his education was not good enough.

23

At age twenty-three, he went into debt to become a partner in a small store. Three years later his business partner died, leaving him a huge debt that took years to repay.

28

At age twenty-eight, after developing a romantic relationship with a young lady for four years, he asked her to marry him. She said "No."

37

At age thirty-seven, on his third try, he was finally elected to Congress. Two years later he ran again and failed to be reelected. It was about this time he had what some today would call a nervous breakdown.

A Baker's Dozen of Helpful Hints

1. Don't play roles.

2. Choose your friends wisely.

3. Don't let things drift.

4. Admit your fears.

5. Make time to get away.

6. Be willing to compromise.

7. Seek a balance in your life.

8. Be realistic.

9. Take one thing at a time.

10. Slow down.

11. Avoid excuses.

12. Talk things over.

13. Work on a realistic self-image.

Adapted from Gary R. Collins, *You Can Profit from Stress* (Santa Ana, Calif.: 1977), 194, 195.

Smoothing the Mid-Life Transition

Interview 1

- What is the single most important thing you have learned during this course?

- What is the biggest challenge that faces you in parenting your teen?

- What is the biggest challenge that faces you in handling mid-life changes?

- What questions still linger in your mind about the material covered in this course?

- How can I best pray for you?

The task of a transition is:

a. To terminate a time in one's life.
b. To accept the loss that the termination entails.
c. To review and evaluate the past.
d. To decide which aspects of the past to keep and which to reject.
e. To consider one's wishes and possibilities for the future.

From D. J. Levinson, C. N. Darrow, E. B. Klein, M. H. Levinson, and B. McKee, *The Seasons of a Man's Life* (New York: Ballantine Books, 1978), 51.

Interview 2

a. What word or phrase would you use to describe the stage of life or transition you are experiencing at this point?

b. In what ways do you experience a sense of loss as your children enter the young adult years? as you leave behind your young adult years?

c. How would you describe your adult life and parenting experience up to this point?

d. How do you feel about the changes that come with a new stage of life?

e. What are some new goals or opportunities you foresee in the future?